EVANGELISTIC GROWTH IN ACTS 1 & 2

D. WADE ARMSTRONG

BROADMAN PRESS
Nashville, Tennessee

© Copyright 1983 • Broadman Press
All rights reserved

4262-42

ISBN: 0-8054-6242-2

Dewey Decimal Classification: 226.6
Subject headings: BIBLE. N.T. ACTS / / EVANGELISTIC WORK

Library of Congress Catalog Card Number: 83-70375

Printed in the United States of America

Dedicated to

SHIRLEY WATSON ARMSTRONG

My Wife
A Gift from God
Best Friend and Wonderful Companion

CONTENTS

FOREWORD

Wade Armstrong is a pastor who understands the biblical concept of evangelism. There are academicians who learn the principles but never have the opportunity to try them. Through more than twenty-five years as a pastor and eighteen years as a director of evangelism and missions, he has experienced the use of these principles.

The biblical principles of evangelism gathered from Dr. Armstrong's analysis of Acts 1 and 2 are easy to read and understand.

The Lord's imperative to make disciples requires that believers present the gospel to the lost everywhere. Jesus laid the foundation for this in his deeds and example. The seven chapters dealing with the foundation clearly state that evangelism is founded in the passion of Jesus and the ground work for evangelistic growth is set in his ministry.

The study in Acts 1 and 2 reveals through Dr. Armstrong that almost every principle of evangelistic growth can be modeled in the early church. In his very unique homiletical-exegetical style he discusses twelve important themes of evangelism. He brings each one into contemporary application. He deals with publicity, personal witnessing, preaching, conviction, salvation, persuasion, profession, security, spiritual power, spiritual gifts, praise, and popularity. Each of these brief succinct messages teaches important lessons that every Christian ought to learn.

This book demonstrates there is a biblical role model for all who are interested in growing an evangelistic church in today's world.

This book is the fruit of a life well spent in local church evangelism and will make a very important contribution to all who read it.

ROBERT L. HAMBLIN
Vice-President, Evangelism
Home Mission Board,
Southern Baptist Convention

INTRODUCTION

There are two types of churches in the world today: churches on maintenance and churches on mission.

Churches on maintenance have settled down to the routine of maintaining services, property, organizational life, and so forth. They are satisfied with a maintenance stance. Maintenance has become their mission.

Churches on mission put evangelistic growth first, in accordance with the command Jesus gave his church. The Great Commission (Matt. 28:19-20) contains only one command: "make disciples." Jesus spoke in the imperative. He was saying, "I really mean this!" The words *going*, *baptizing*, and *teaching* are participles in Greek, the original language of the New Testament. Greeks didn't give commands in participles.

A church on mission is going, baptizing, and teaching as a means of carrying out Christ's command and first priority: making disciples.

It was no happenstance that evangelistic growth in the first century was rapid and lasting. It is no accident today when a church grows rapidly. When the biblical principles of evangelistic growth are enacted with boldness from the Holy Spirit, notable church growth will occur.

In this book the biblical principles of evangelistic growth are examined in the same sequence as found in Acts 1 and 2.

Part I

The Background
of Biblical Principles
# of Evangelistic Growth

1

The Beginning of Evangelistic Growth

During his ministry, Christ repeatedly stressed the importance of evangelism: presenting the gospel to the lost. There were five occasions (other than the Great Commission) when he put evangelism first.

First, at the beginning of his ministry Christ said, "Follow me, and I will make you fishers of men" (Matt. 4:19). This was a promise. If a church does not make fishing for men its priority, is it really following Christ?

Second, when his ministry was about two thirds over, Christ announced his purpose for his church. It was to "loose on earth" those who were bound by sin (Matt. 16:13-20).

Third, shortly before he died, Christ paused in Jericho and led a tax collector to salvation. Then he announced his life's purpose: "For the Son of Man has come to seek and to save that which was lost" (Luke 19:10). Christ's purpose surely should be the purpose of his church.

Fourth, on his resurrection day Christ told his followers, "As the Father has sent Me, I also send you" (John 20:21). His purpose for coming into the world is our purpose for going out into the world.

On the same occasion Christ told them what should be the content of a witness about him: "that the Christ should suffer and rise again from the dead the third day; and that repentance for forgiveness of sins should be proclaimed in

His name to all the nations, beginning from Jerusalem.
You are witnesses of these things" (Luke 24:46-48).

Fifth, the day he ascended to the Father, Christ took his
last opportunity to prioritize evangelistic growth. He said,
"You shall be My witnesses . . . to the remotest part of the
earth" (Acts 1:8). This command was the last recorded
thing Christ said before he ascended.

If your mother called you to her deathbed and said,
"This is the last thing I will ask of you," you would regard
her statement seriously.

The First Church Prioritized Evangelistic Growth

The early believers accepted Jesus' priority as their
priority. This was reflected in the rapidity with which they
won others. The reported evangelistic growth in Jerusalem
was fantastic. At first there was "a gathering of about one
hundred and twenty persons" (Acts 1:15). Ten days later
they were filled with the Holy Spirit and began to witness.
On one day they grew by "about three thousand souls"
(Acts 2:41). From 120 to 3,000 in ten days was evangelistic
growth par excellence.

A few days later, Peter and John preached to a crowd in
the Temple area, and "many of those who had heard the
message believed; and the number of men came to be
about five thousand" (Acts 4:4).

Satan used persecution in an attempt to stop the
evangelistic growth. But a renewed surge of Spirit-filled
"boldness" came upon the believers (Acts 4:31). They
witnessed of the living Christ with such great results that
they stopped counting the converts. The Scriptures describe their number as "the multitude of them that believed" (Acts 4:32, KJV).

A short time later there was another surge of evangelistic
growth. Satan again tried to stop the growth. He enticed a

couple to lie about money. But the Lord promptly dispatched them through death (Acts 5:1-13). "And all the more believers in the Lord, multitudes of men and women, were constantly added to their number" (Acts 5:14).

Their rapid evangelistic growth is presented in the Scriptures as the accepted norm: "And in those days . . . the number of the disciples was multipled" (Acts 6:1, KJV).

One of the most astounding accounts of the church's rapid growth concerns the widespread conversion of Jewish priests: "A great many of the priests were becoming obedient to the faith" (Acts 6:7). This is amazing! The priests usually were Sadducees, a Jewish sect that did not believe in the resurrection.[1]

The historian, Josephus, reports that there were about 20,000 priests who worked in and out of the city of Jerusalem.[2] Perhaps 5,000 or more were saved.

A summary of evangelistic growth in the Jerusalem church states, "The Lord added to their number day by day" (Acts 2:47, RSV).

When most of the church was driven from Jerusalem, "[they] went about preaching the word" (Acts 8:4). Here the Greek word for *preaching* means evangelism, or gospel. The members were evangelizing everywhere they went.

When Philip preached Christ in the city of Samaria, "the multitudes . . . were giving attention" (Acts 8:6). Later, in Joppa, "many believed in the Lord" (Acts 9:42). In Antioch, "a large number . . . believed" (Acts 11:21).

The devil again tried to stop the evangelistic growth. He led Herod to kill James and attempt to kill Peter. God thwarted Satan. The triumph is reflected in this statement, "But the word of the Lord continued to grow and to be multiplied" (Acts 12:24).

As the gospel moved farther into the Roman Empire, we

read accounts of evangelistic growth such as these: "Nearly the whole city assembled to hear the word of God" (Acts 13:44); "the word of the Lord was being spread through the whole region" (Acts 13:49); and "a great multitude believed" (Acts 14:1).

The devil tried to stop the evangelistic growth in Asia Minor by raising a controversy among the churches about circumcision and salvation (Acts 15:1-2). When this was settled, the evangelistic growth was so strong that churches "were increasing in number daily" (Acts 16:5).

When the gospel spread into Europe, churches sprang up and grew rapidly with both Jewish and Greek members. "And some of them [Jews] were persuaded . . . along with a great multitude of . . . Greeks. . . . Many . . . when they heard were believing and being baptized" (Acts 17:4; 18:8).

A summary statement reveals that rapid growth continued both in Europe and Asia Minor. "So the word of the Lord was growing mightily and prevailing" (Acts 19:20).

Why did the first churches grow so rapidly? The answer is found in the principles of evangelistic growth which they believed and practiced. These principles surface in the first two chapters of Acts, as the account of the growth of the first church begins to unfold.

Part II

The Foundation Principles of Evangelistic Growth

2

The Passion of the Son

The first principle of evangelistic growth, believed in and proclaimed by the early church, is Jesus Christ's death and resurrection for the salvation of sinners (Acts 2:23-24; Rom. 4:25).

The Scripture says Christ "shewed himself alive after his passion" (Acts 1:3, KJV). The word *passion* in Greek means "to suffer." When applied to Christ, it also means "to die." This is made clearer in the verse stating that he was made "for a little while lower than the angels, namely Jesus, because of the suffering of death" (Heb. 2:9).

The first church made Christ's death and resurrection the bottom line of their faith. In proclaiming Jesus to the lost multitudes, they started with the truth of his death and resurrection. The result was evangelistic growth. No church can experience evangelistic growth without proclaiming the crucified, risen Savior.

Certainty in Their Minds

The first Christians believed that Christ had died for each of them personally. Peter wrote, "He himself bore our sins in his body on the cross" (1 Pet. 2:24). They believed that the sins of each person put Christ on the cross. Peter told the Pentecostal crowd: "This Man . . . you nailed to a cross . . . and put Him to death" (Acts 2:23).

The disciples knew Christ had died. Some had been at

the cross (Matt. 27:45). Matthew wrote about some dramatic happenings. "And behold, the veil of the temple was torn in two from top to bottom, and the earth shook; and the rocks were split, and the tombs were opened" (Matt. 27:51-52).

The disciples were sure about Christ's resurrection. Peter proclaimed, "This Jesus God raised up again, to which we are all witnesses" (Acts 2:32).

The resurrection was an incredible event. "Many bodies of the saints who had fallen asleep were raised; and coming out of the tombs after His resurrection they entered the holy city and appeared to many" (Matt. 27:52-53). Don't you know that woke some people! People today need to be awakened to the fact that Jesus Christ is alive. We need to obey the angel's command given at Christ's tomb: "Go quickly and tell . . . that He has risen from the dead" (Matt. 28:7).

The first disciples believed Christ was alive, because they had personal experiences with him. A. T. Robertson said, "The early disciples including Paul never doubted the fact of the Resurrection, once they were convinced by personal experience."[1]

The first disciples were certain of three things about Christ's death. First, they knew Christ died voluntarily (John 10:18). Peter declared that Jesus had died "by the predetermined plan and foreknowledge of God" (Acts 2:23).

Second, the early believers were certain that Jesus had died vicariously. *Vicariously* means "for me." He became sin for us (2 Cor. 5:21).

Third, they knew that Jesus died victoriously. The Scriptures say Christ "Yielded up His spirit" (Matt. 27:50). This means he sent back his spirit to his father of his own accord.[2] Jesus cried out as he died, "It is finished" (John

19:30). It was the shout of a victor who had won his last engagement with the enemy.[3]

Jesus had announced his resurrection when he said, "Destroy this Temple, and in three days I will raise it up" (John 2:19). So, the early believers preached that the death of Christ was in the eternal purpose of God. He was as "the Lamb slain from the foundation of the world" (Rev. 13:8, KJV).

A Centrality in Their Message

The day Christ arose he gave his followers the centrality of their witness. He told them their witness had a divine side ("Christ should suffer and rise again from the dead"), and a human side ("that repentance for forgiveness of sins should be proclaimed in His name to all the nations"). Jesus underscored this as the focal point of their message by adding, "You are witnesses of these things" (Luke 24:46-48).

The disciples understood the centrality of the message. Peter gave both the divine and human elements of the witness: "You nailed [Jesus] to a cross. . . . And God raised Him up again. . . . Repent, . . . for the forgiveness of your sins" (Acts 2:23-24,38). Peter and John told a crowd at the Temple, "You . . . put to death the Prince of Life, the one whom God raised from the dead. . . . Repent therefore and return, that your sins may be wiped away" (Acts 3:15,19).

In court they boldly testified: "whom you crucified, whom God raised from the dead" (Acts 4:1-10). When the apostles were taken before the Jewish Council, they testified, "God . . . raised up Jesus, whom you had put to death. . . . He is the one . . . to grant repentance . . . and forgiveness of sins. And we are witnesses of these things" (Acts 5:27-32). Stephen, in his last sermon, preached the death and resurrection of Jesus (Acts 7:51-56).

As the gospel moved outside Jerusalem, Philip explained the death and resurrection of Christ to an Ethiopian (Acts 8:32-35). Peter gave the same witness to the Gentile, Cornelius (Acts 10:39-40).

When the gospel spread into Asia Minor, the message remained the same: the death and resurrection of Jesus Christ (Acts 13:28-30). When the gospel reached Europe, the witness continued: "Christ had to suffer and rise again from the dead" (Acts 17:3).

The Scriptures make the content of the gospel witness crystal clear: "Christ died for our sins, . . . He was raised, . . . He appeared" (1 Cor. 15:3-5). According to the Scriptures, this witness is "the message," "the word of God," "the word of the gospel" (Acts 4:4; 4:31; 13:5; 14:3; 15:7). The core of the Word is the death and resurrection of Christ. Evangelistic growth is certain when the centrality of the witness is boldly proclaimed (Acts 2:37-41; 5:32; 1 Thess. 1:5).

Churches can't have evangelistic growth when the people think witnessing means attending church regularly, paying their bills, living clean lives, not telling dirty jokes, and tithing. These people have substituted activities, that even lost people can do, for telling the saving message of Christ.

Likewise, a church will not grow if it is led by people who believe evangelism means doing nice and needed things for others. If that were so, everywhere the Red Cross works evangelistic growth would occur. Evangelism should include social ministries. Evangelistic growth will follow if the social ministries are perfc ned for the purpose of telling people about Jesus.

The evangel, or gospel, is the good news about Jesus' death, resurrection, and saving power. An evangelist is one who tells the good news about Christ from his own experience. Evangelism is employing biblical principles and human methods to confront people with Christ.

A Circumference to Their Mission

The early believers had to decide to whom they would go with the good news. Jesus assigned the whole world to his followers when he said, "Make disciples of all the nations" (Matt. 28:19). Jesus stated the circumference of the message in his last words, "You shall be My witnesses both in Jerusalem, and all of Judea and Samaria, and even to the remotest part of the earth" (Acts 1:8).

In Jerusalem

With the infilling of the Holy Spirit, the early believers began to witness in Jerusalem. Various writers estimate that as many as 50,000 people were led to Christ before persecution scattered the church.

In All Judea and Samaria

Fifteen or more nations were represented at Pentecost, but they were slow to take the gospel outside Jerusalem. Like the first church, today's churches have been assigned the whole world. Race, color, creed, and all barriers need to be crossed with the gospel. Evangelistic growth needs to be commensurate with, and even surpass, population growth. It took persecution in Jerusalem to get the first church to go to Samaria and beyond. What will it take to move churches in America into evangelistic growth among all people?

After the persecution, the gospel went to Egypt through the Ethiopian whom Philip won to Christ (Acts 8:26-36). Peter, after much persuasion from the Lord, preached to the Gentile, Cornelius (Acts 10:1-48). Slowly, the gospel began to spread to those outside the Jewish religion. The movement was sluggish because "those who were scattered because of the persecution . . . made their way . . . speaking the word to no one except to Jews alone" (Acts 11:19).

The Holy Spirit led the church in Antioch to send Barnabas and Paul to Asia Minor (Acts 13:1-4). They first spoke to Jews, but the Jews rejected the gospel. Then Paul said, "It was necessary that the word of God should be spoken to you first; since you repudiate it, and judge yourselves unworthy of eternal life, behold, we are turning to the Gentiles" (Acts 13:46).

The Remotest Part of the Earth

A few days before Jesus died, several Greeks expressed a desire to see him. He took that opportunity to tell his followers, "And I, if I am lifted up from the earth, will draw all men to Myself" (John 12:32). As believers took the gospel to Asia Minor and Europe, churches experienced evangelistic growth. Also, "the churches . . . were increasing in number daily" (Acts 16:5).

At a national missions conference, I heard that places where evangelistic growth is taking place are places where new churches are being formed.

The Message Symbolized

Christ regarded his death and resurrection so importantly, he symbolized them. He instituted his Supper to represent his death (Matt. 26:26-28) and baptism (Matt. 28:19), which represents his burial and resurrection (Rom. 6:4-6). The irreducible witness for a church that wants to experience evangelistic growth is: Christ died; Christ rose; and Christ has the power to save sinners (Heb. 7:25-26).

3

The Promise of the Father

Shortly before Jesus returned to heaven he told his disciples "to wait for what the Father had promised" (Acts 1:4). Jesus was telling them that they could trust the Father. Whatever he promised he would do. Do you believe you can rely upon what the Father promises? Those early believers did. It made a difference in their lives and their evangelistic endeavor.

Promise Validated the Purpose of the Father

Christ told the disciples that the Father's promise was "you shall be baptized with the Holy Spirit" (Acts 1:5). If the disciples were to stand with any assurance, they had to believe in the Father's promise. The Son, their Savior, was about to return to heaven. Yet, it was the Father's purpose that they not be left alone. Their evangelistic task was too great for them to do alone. "For their difficult work the apostles needed a personal equipment."[1] The personal Helper was the Holy Spirit.

Jesus had told them to make disciples of all nations. Now he was telling them that for this work they had a need in their lives which only the Father could supply. John the Baptist had "baptized with water" (Acts 1:5), an act whereby they publicly committed themselves to the kingdom of God. For the work of the kingdom, the baptism of the Holy Spirit was supremely important. W. O.

Carver says that this baptism "means burial and saturation of the personality in the influence and control of God so that the human person and the divine work together."[2] The Father would make them effective witnesses.

Jesus told the disciples to wait for the promises. The tense he used meant "keep on waiting." The promise was so important they were to wait with expectancy and alertness.

The Promise Established the Position of the Saved

Jesus didn't say to pray for the baptism of the Holy Spirit. He said to wait for it. Today we do not have to wait for this baptism. It occurs simultaneously with the new-birth experience. To be baptized by the Holy Spirit is the same as being born of the Spirit (John 3:6). The Scriptures teach that every believer has been baptized by the Holy Spirit. "For by one Spirit we were all baptized into one body, . . . and we were all made to drink of one Spirit" (1 Cor. 12:13). This Scripture puts the baptism in the past tense. This is how we entered the body of Christ. We were placed there by the Holy Spirit upon repentance of sin and faith in Christ as Savior.

The baptism of the Holy Spirit makes the position of the saved greater than that known by the prophets, including John the Baptist (Matt. 11:11). Through the baptism of the Holy Spirit, the saved have an artesian well of spiritual life constantly bubbling up within them (John 7:37-39). Once one is baptized by the Holy Spirit, he is never spiritually thirsty again (John 4:14).

The Promise Personified the Son

The Holy Spirit is the embodiment of the Son in the believer. To have the baptism of the Holy Spirit is to have Christ.

When Jesus told his disciples he was going to leave them, he said, "And I will ask the Father, and He will give you another Helper" (John 14:16). The word *another* means one of the same kind as Jesus. In fact, the Holy Spirit so closely identifies with Jesus that he is also called "Spirit of Jesus" (Acts 16:6-7). It is through the Holy Spirit that Jesus keeps his promise to always be with us.

The work of the Holy Spirit is to show us the Son. Jesus said of him, "He shall glorify me" (John 16:14). The word *me* is emphatic. It means "me and no one else he shall glorify." This means the Holy Spirit never calls attention to himself but always to Jesus. Therefore, anyone who emphasizes the Holy Spirit more than he emphasizes Jesus is not led of the Spirit.[3]

About his going away Jesus said, "I will not leave you as orphans; I will come to you" (John 14:18). God has no orphans. If you have been given the new birth by the baptism of the Holy Spirit, you are a child of God. Through Jesus Christ you have direct access to him.

When Jesus ascended, the Holy Spirit descended. Through the Holy Spirit we have Christ present with us. He kept his promise. We are not alone; we are not orphans.

The Holy Spirit points us to Jesus and helps us to point others to Jesus. He always magnifies Jesus.

The Promise Brings the Presence of the Holy Spirit

The Holy Spirit is present with the believer as a person. He is the third person of the Godhead (Matt. 28:19). As a person he is our "Helper" (John 14:16). This means he stands by us and moves along with us. The Holy Spirit is so real Jesus used the personal pronoun "he" six times in succession to describe him (John 16:13).

Evangelistic growth comes only from the presence and

work of the Holy Spirit in and through the church. The Scriptures say that the church all over Judea, Galilee, and Samaria "continued to increase," because "it was going on in the fear of the Lord and in the comfort of the Holy Spirit" (Acts 9:31). The word *comfort* is the same word that Jesus used for the Holy Spirit as being the "Helper" (John 14:16). He was undergirding the church. That's why it continued to have evangelistic growth.

Our hope for spiritual awakening and evangelistic growth lies in our permitting the Holy Spirit to control us. He speaks about Jesus and also empowers us to speak about him (John 15:26-27).

The Father could not have made a more important promise than the baptism of the Holy Spirit. Since the Day of Pentecost every believer has had the Holy Spirit living within (1 Cor. 6:19). He gives spiritual insight and helps us witness to others about Christ.

4

The Power of the Holy Spirit

During a flight from Los Angeles to New York, an explosion blew a motor out of the fuselage. The lights went out, and the plane dipped dangerously. The pilot and copilot worked desperately, righted the plane, and headed for Denver. The electrical and hydraulic power were practically gone. When the plane finally landed, someone asked the pilot, "How did you manage to land safely?"

The pilot replied, "In a situation like that, you just let God take over."

Jesus was about to leave his disciples when they desperately needed help. He had told them to make disciples of all nations. To enable them to do this Christ said, "But you shall receive power when the Holy Spirit has come upon you" (Acts 1:8).

The disciples needed power. One of them had denied Christ. The others had fled in fear.

Even Jesus had needed the power of the Holy Spirit in his earthly ministry. The Spirit came upon Jesus at his baptism (John 1:32). "He returned to Galilee in the power of the Spirit" (Luke 4:14).

If Jesus depended upon the Holy Spirit, we must. W. A. Criswell says, "Through the ages any mighty work for God ever done, has been done in the power of the Holy Spirit. To be a child of God is not enough. We must also be endowed from God for the work committed for us. We must possess divine enablement."[1]

Power Promised by Christ

The night before Jesus died, he told his disciples "It is to your advantage that I go away; for if I do not go away, the Helper shall not come to you" (John 16:7).

On his resurrection day, Jesus told his disciples that they were to witness of his death, his resurrection, and his authority to forgive the sins of those who repented. Then he added, "But you are to stay in the city until you are clothed with power from on high" (Luke 24:49).

On his Ascension Day, Christ gave his disciples his promise, "But you shall receive power" (Acts 1:8). This promise was fulfilled ten days later when "they were all filled with the Holy Spirit" (Acts 2:4).

The promise of power was for all of Christ's followers. When he said "you," he wasn't limiting his promise just to the first disciples. The promise was also for all who will become Christians. Peter told lost people that if they would turn away from their sins they would have forgiveness and "receive the gift of the Holy Spirit" (Acts 2:38).

Christ told us when the power of the Holy Spirit would be ours, "But you shall receive power when the Holy Spirit has come upon you" (Acts 1:8).

Therefore, a believer is not to pray for power. He already has power, for he has the Holy Spirit. He dwells in the believer (Rom. 8:9). We should pray that we will be open channels for the power of the Holy Spirit to work through us.

During World War II, King George VI was preparing to make a radio broadcast. A few minutes before broadcast time, a break occurred in the electrical system. An engineer found the faulty conductor, but there was no time to replace it. He bridged the gap with his hands. The current was channeled through him, and the world heard the king's message.

The King of kings wants to channel his message through us. He makes it possible by giving us the power of his Holy Spirit.

Power is in a Person

The Holy Spirit is not "it." He's the third person of the Trinity. The Holy Spirit has divine attributes. The Holy Spirit as a divine person has complete power. The person of the Holy Spirit is living in us. We have his power for evangelistic growth.

Before Jesus came his Word announced the source of spiritual power: "'Not by might nor by power, but by My Spirit,' says the Lord of hosts" (Zech. 4:6). We must make plans and use methods in evangelism, but we must not depend upon them to bring spiritual results.

Personal witnessing and preaching are methods for evangelistic growth. Nowhere, however, does God tell us to rely upon them for spiritual power and results.

In evangelistic growth we must not even trust in prayer for spiritual effectiveness. We must pray. Prayer is our effective instrument in evangelistic growth, but we must not trust in prayer alone. We must trust in the Holy Spirit.

The disciples were unable to do effective personal witnessing or public preaching until the outpouring of the Holy Spirit. Any effectiveness today in our preaching and witnessing lies in the divine gift from heaven. The person of the Holy Spirit is the dynamic force in evangelism.

We can permit the Holy Spirit to demonstrate his power through us. Paul said, "And my message and my preaching were . . . in demonstration of the Spirit and of power" (1 Cor. 2:4). For the Holy Spirit to demonstrate his power through us we must let him control us. We are commanded to keep on being filled with the Holy Spirit (Eph. 5:18). This means we are to keep on being controlled by him.

The early believers were repeatedly filled with the Holy Spirit (Acts 2:4; 4:31). To be effective we must do the same. With our trust in God we should use plans and methods for evangelistic growth.

The Purpose of the Power

Christ made it very clear that he would send the Holy Spirit to help us witness. He said, "You shall receive power; . . . and you shall be My witnesses" (Acts 1:8). The Holy Spirit can use our witness for evangelistic growth. He can take the most timid witnesses and give them boldness. "For the Spirit that God has given us does not make us timid; instead, His Spirit fills us with power, love, and self-control. Do not be ashamed, then, of witnessing for our Lord" (2 Tim. 1:7-8, GNB). Since the Holy Spirit does not make us timid, we should not be timid. Satan wants to use our timidity to keep us from witnessing.

There are three tests that will tell you if you are filled or controlled by the Holy Spirit.

First, do you love all people? Love can be fully expressed only by the power of the Holy Spirit.

Second, do you give money freely and liberally to the Lord through his church? This kind of giving can be done with the power of the Holy Spirit.

Third, do you witness to the lost? Do you tell others that Christ died for them, that he arose, and that he has power to forgive their sins? Do you tell your own experience with Jesus to verify that you know him? This type of biblical witnessing can be done only by the power of the Holy Spirit.

Jesus said of the Holy Spirit, "He will bear witness of Me," and "He shall glorify Me" (John 15:26, 16:14). This means the Holy Spirit tells others about Jesus. He does it through us (Acts 5:32).

A pastor sent people to do evangelistic visitation. Teams kept telling about a man who was skeptical. They were unable to answer his questions. Christ didn't seem to make any impression on him.

The pastor finally decided to visit him. When he told him he was the pastor, the man said, "Oh, you are the one who has been sending those people to see me. Come on in here." The man began to ask piercing questions and propose skeptical ideas. The pastor was highly trained, and he soon backed the man into an intellectual corner. However, he didn't win him to Christ.

The next visitation night a humble deacon requested the man's name. The pastor started to refuse, but decided it could do no harm. When the deacon introduced himself, the man immediately started asking his skeptical questions and making cutting remarks about Christ. He went so far as to tell the deacon that he thought Christ was illegitimate.

The man suddenly stopped talking, because the deacon was crying. He said, "Oh, I'm sorry. I've hurt your feelings. I shouldn't have done that. At least you thought enough of me to come here. I'm sorry if something I said about you hurt."

The deacon replied, "You haven't said anything about me that hurt. What you've said about my dear Savior has hurt deeply. You see, he died for me. He arose from the dead, and he came into my heart when I turned away from my sins. He has forgiven me. He is with me every day, and he is preparing a home for me in heaven. I love him so very much, because he first loved me."

The skeptic was silent for a moment. Then he said, "Deacon, if Christ is that real to you, he must really be the Savior. Will you kneel with me and tell him that I give him my life right now?"

The Scripture says that when the Jewish leaders observed the boldness of Peter and John, they marveled. Then they remembered that these men had been associated with Jesus (Acts 4:13). The Holy Spirit can also endow us with boldness for witnessing.

In the Jerusalem church, evangelistic outreach grew when the people asked the Lord for boldness in witnessing. The Lord promptly answered, and "They were all filled with the Holy Spirit, and began to speak the Word of God with boldness" (Acts 4:31).

Do you pray for boldness in witnessing? Does your church?

Let's pray for a mighty moving of God's Holy Spirit. Let's pray for a great spiritual awakening. God's promise of power still stands, "Call to Me, and I will answer you, and I will tell you great and mighty things, which you do not know" (Jer. 33:3).

5

The Proclamation of the Angels

As Jesus ascended into heaven, two angels made this proclamation: "This Jesus, who has been taken up from you into heaven, will come in just the same way" (Acts 1:11). This doctrine of the second coming of Christ is part of the evangelistic message.

Two words in one verse teach the second coming. "And then that lawless one . . . the Lord will slay . . . and bring to an end by the appearance of His coming" (2 Thess. 2:8). The word *appearing* (Epiphany) is used several times in the New Testament for the second coming of Christ. However, the most prevalently used word is *coming* (Parousia).[1]

The Greeks used the term *appearing*, which means "the breaking forth," to describe the dramatic appearance of a god or gods.[2] Paul used the term to say that the real God is coming back. The term *coming* was familiar to the Hebrews and was used among them to announce the return of Christ. The word *Parousia*, or coming, is from two words which mean "to be with." Christ is coming, and we will be with him.

Negative Results from Proclamation

Negative results for evangelistic growth can result from improperly teaching his coming. The New Testament gives at least five.

First is the teaching that Christ will set up a military-political kingdom. This was the view of Christ's apostles when they asked, "Lord, is it at this time You are restoring the kingdom to Israel?" (Acts 1:6). The action of the words shows that they kept on asking. Christ rebuked them in saying that long periods and points in time were under the sovereignty of the Father.[3]

Second, setting a time for Christ's coming is incorrect. Christ said it was not for us to know the time; only the Father knows (Matt. 24:36). Christ turned his disciples' interest from predictions of time about the kingdom to the proclamation of the gospel of the kingdom.[4]

Third, the tendency to just wait for his coming, instead of doing the work of the kingdom until he comes, hinders evangelistic growth. The angels asked the disciples why they stood gazing after Jesus. They were saying, "Why don't you get busy witnessing, as the Lord commanded?"

Fourth, the false teaching that Christ has already returned stops evangelistic growth. Christ warned about this (Matt. 24:5-26).

Fifth, when the teaching about Christ's return becomes the main emphasis in a church, evangelistic growth eventually ceases. I know a church where the pastor made this doctrine central. The growth of the church deteriorated rapidly. Second Thessalonians seems to warn not to over-emphasize the second coming.

Encouragement to the Saved

There is a very positive side to the second coming of Christ.

First, it is the happy hope of a Christian (Titus 2:13). A Christian can look to a glorious day when Christ will climax history.

Second, the promise of his return encourages the believer to witness. Christ said his gospel would be preached "for a witness to all, . . . and then the end shall come" (Matt. 24:14).

Third, Christ's coming is an incentive to holy living. This will hasten the coming (2 Pet. 3:11-12).

Fourth, the Christian can know that Christ will return victoriously and consummate the age (Matt. 25:31-32; 1 Cor. 15-24). This should inspire us to bring more to Christ, to share the victory.

Fifth, the fact that we are going to get to personally see Jesus upon his return should inspire us in evangelistic growth (Matt. 24:30; 1 John 3:2).

Sixth, knowing that Christ is coming can inspire the Christian to stay close to him so that he will not be ashamed at Christ's coming (1 John 2:28).

Warning to the Lost

The second coming of Christ can bring unspeakable joy to the saved; it can bring abject terror to the lost. The Bible gives the following warnings to the lost:

First, they must be saved before Christ returns (Heb. 9:27-28).

Second, at Christ's coming lost people will stand before him in judgment and receive a sentence of eternal punishment (Matt. 25:41,46).

Third, the certainty of Christ's return is a call for lost people to repent now (2 Pet. 3:9).

Fourth, Christ's return will be unexpected. He will come like a thief and with sudden destruction (1 Thess. 5:2-3; Matt. 24:37-44; 2 Pet. 3:10).

Fifth, lost people should not scoff at the eminence of Christ's return nor presume upon the Lord's patience (2 Pet. 3:9; Rom. 2:4).

Christ taught the certainty of his coming. The angels' proclamation adds to that certainty. The early believers engaged in evangelistic growth in the light of the certainty (Acts 3:17-21).

For expected evangelistic growth today, we must proclaim at least three truths about his coming: he is coming; we don't know when; we should be ready now!

6

The Propensity Toward Unity

There was a national disposition toward unity in the first church. They were "all with one accord" (Acts 1:14). Their unity highly affected their evangelistic growth.

The New Testament word translated *one accord* comes from a double word that means of the same mind or same spirit. Except for Romans 15:6 it is found only in Acts. Yet, it occurs there eleven times. The word denotes their inner unity. It speaks of doing things unanimously or with one spirit.

The oneness of the first church is stressed by R. B. Rackham in his book, *The Acts of the Apostles*. He states, "The most characteristic words in the early chapters of the Acts are *all, with one accord, together*."[1]

Importance of Unity in Evangelistic Growth

Unity among God's people seems to have a threefold effect upon evangelistic growth.

First, the Holy Spirit can work freely through the people when they are in one accord. Scripture unites the "fellowship of the Spirit, . . . [and] being of the same mind" (Phil. 2:1-2).

Where there's unity among God's people, the Holy Spirit is not so likely to be quenched or grieved (1 Thess. 5:19; Eph. 4:30). The Holy Spirit must be allowed to work if there are to be evangelistic results.

Second, the unity of a church affects the witnessing of

the saved. People who have animosity and unforgiveness cannot witness effectively to the lost.

Third, the salvation of the lost is highly dependent upon the unity of the church. When word spreads over a community that a church is having a fight, lost people stay away. Even when they attend, they can sense the coldness and the lack of love.

In a booklet *Churches Alive and Growing*, Frank Crumpler gives some steps for effecting evangelistic growth in the church. One is to create a loving atmosphere of Christian concern among the people. "In congregations where there is harmony, there's usually growth. . . . A church with a compassion for lost souls usually has a harmonious membership."[2]

Fourth, a spirit of one accord in a church will help to make the worship services celebrative and contagious. In congregations where the people are "of the same mind with one another" and glorify God "with one accord . . . [and] with one voice," people in large numbers are more likely to receive the Lord Jesus Christ (Rom. 15:5-6).

Three times in succession the Scriptures show the positive effect of a harmonious congregation upon the salvation of the multitudes (Acts 2:46-47; 4:24,32-33; 5:12-14).

The adverse effect of the lack of harmony upon evangelistic growth becomes strikingly clear in a story about a church that split over whether to buy a new organ or a new piano. Feelings ran high. Discussions became heated. Finally they voted to buy both. In about two weeks the piano disappeared. Seven years later it was found, in the baptistry.

The Basis of Unity

Since unity is so important for evangelistic growth, let's consider the scriptural basis for unity among God's people.

Knowing Christ is the first basis for unity. The Scripture says we are all one in Christ (Gal. 3:28).

Prioritizing Christ's Great Commission is the second basis for unity. The members of the first church were united in their purpose to witness. Instead of silence about Jesus, with one accord they prayed for boldness to speak his message (Acts 4:24-33).

When a murmuring arose in the first church (Acts 6:1-7), it was handled quickly. It appeared that the leaders had agreed ahead of time to work together. Because of their single-minded purpose to win others to Christ, they refused to permit dissension to interfere with the ministry of the Word. As a result, the disciples continued to increase greatly in Jerusalem, and even a great many of the priests were saved (Acts 6:7).

Love is the third basis for unity. People who love Christ, each other, and the lost have a solid basis for unity.

Jesus said he had a new commandment for us. It was that we should love one another. He said that by our loving one another all men would know that we belonged to him (John 13:34-35). Christ asked the Father to make us one (John 17:20-23). We are told to "put on love, which is the perfect bond of unity" (Col. 3:14).

Forgiveness is the fourth basis of unity in the church. Christ taught us to forgive as we are forgiven. He also said if we don't forgive, we won't be forgiven (Matt. 6:14-15). Christ tied forgiveness to evangelistic growth (Matt. 18:15-18).

The Scriptures teach a church should be forgiving and united. Without forgiveness and harmony, Satan will take advantage of the situation (1 Cor. 1:9-10; 2 Cor. 2:10-11).

The fifth basis for unity is the infilling of the Holy Spirit. Christians are instructed "to preserve the unity of the Spirit in the bond of peace" (Eph. 4:3). The Holy Spirit enables evangelistic growth. If he is quenched, the growth is quenched.

An agreement upon the content of the gospel is the sixth basis of unity for evangelistic growth. The first churches disagreed about whether one had to be circumcised to be a Christian. Evangelistic growth seemed hindered until the question was settled. There was a "one accord" vote by the leaders to add nothing to the gospel (Acts 15:1-29).

When the result of the vote was carried to the scattered churches, they were "strengthened in the faith, and were increasing in number daily" (Acts 16:5).

Think what could happen in evangelistic growth if all of God's people would agree to be agreeable and make evangelistic growth their first priority.

7

The Prayer of the People

Accurate, reliable information is needed when a thesis is written. You go to the original sources. If churches and Christians today are to have power for evangelistic growth, we must go to the original source of prayer.

It should come as no surprise that the first believers, who prayed much, witnessed with great power. This resulted in evangelistic growth.

Great evangelistic churches are praying churches. Strong Christians are praying Christians. A prayerless life and a prayerless church produce little spiritual growth and evangelistic results.

A. J. Gordon reportedly said that the greatest thing anyone can do for God and man is to pray. Andrew Murray said that the man who mobilizes the church to pray will make the greatest contribution to evangelism.

Prayer for Evangelistic Growth in the Early Church

The members of the first church were people of prayer. "These all with one mind were continually devoting themselves to prayer" (Acts 1:14).

First, they all prayed. It is no marvel that something great happened. Great things would happen in any church if every member prayed.

The word used for prayer means "a pouring out." They

were not just saying words; they were pouring out to the Lord.

Christ had taught them to pray by word and by example. They had seen him pray at his baptism, in the wilderness, on the mountain, alone, in a group, all night, at his transfiguration, the last night before his death, and while dying on the cross (Luke 3:21; 5:16; 6:12, 9:18,29; 11:2; 22:41; 23:46).

Christ taught them "that at all times they ought to pray and not to lose heart" (Luke 18:1). They could have easily lost hope between Christ's ascension and the coming of the Holy Spirit. However, they remembered that he had said, "But you are to stay in the city until you are clothed with power from on high" (Luke 24:49).

Second, the first believers prayed with one mind or with one accord. Their common purpose was to receive the Holy Spirit. They knew they could not carry out Christ's command to evangelize the world in their own power. Perhaps they were also praying for more workers, as Christ had taught (Matt. 9:38).

They prayed for wisdom to select the right person to take Judas' place (Acts 1:24). I'd like to believe they also prayed for relatives, friends, and acquaintances who did not know Christ as the Messiah.

W. A. Criswell told of urging the congregation in an evangelistic crusade to pray for the lost. At the end of the service a man approached Criswell and said, "Didn't you tell us to pray for the lost?"

Criswell replied in the affirmative. The man held out a big, black Bible and said, "All right, show me the chapter and verse."

Criswell said his mind was completely blank; he couldn't think of one verse. The fellow said, "Uh huh, that's what I thought." Then he put his Bible under his arm, turned, and strode triumphantly out.

Criswell said he went to his motel room, slumped down in a chair, and said, "Lord, didn't you say somewhere in your Word that we should pray for the lost?"

He said it seemed that a Presence entered the room. He even felt a tap on his shoulder and heard a voice that said, "My child, have you never read Romans 10:1 that says, 'Brethren, my heart's desire and my prayer to God for them is for their salvation.'"

As they continued in prayer, the first church taught all the new converts to pray (Acts 2:42). The church was told by the Jews to keep silent about Jesus. They prayed for boldness and were filled with the Holy Spirit. Then they went out and spoke the message boldly (Acts 4:29-31).

When a murmuring arose in the church and evangelistic growth was imperiled, the apostles turned the matter over to seven Spirit-filled men. They said, "We will devote ourselves to prayer, and to the ministry of the word" (Acts 6:4). Because they would not stop praying and presenting the message of Christ, "the Word of God kept on spreading; and the number of the disciples continued to increase greatly" (Acts 6:7).

The biblical records on prayer, and the present records I am hearing about, indicate that there is a definite link between evangelistic growth and the prayers of God's people.

Stephen died praying for lost people (Acts 7:59-60). Because the church was "earnest" in prayer, Peter was released from prison (Acts 12:5).

When the Antioch church prayed, the Holy Spirit sent out missionaries from their midst. This resulted in many more being saved (Acts 13:1-4). When Paul and Silas prayed in jail, the jailer and his whole household were saved (Acts 16:25-34).

This is the prayer story of the first church. They prayed fervently. They received new infillings from the Holy Spirit. Great evangelistic growth took place.

Prayer in Evangelistic Growth Today

C. E. Autrey says that the coming of the Holy Spirit made the early church invincible. But prayer preceded it. He further states that prayer is always essential. A prayerless church is an impotent church. No amount of organization and activity can produce spiritual results. Only God can.[1]

We are instructed in the Word to pray for boldness in God's preachers (Eph. 6:18-20); for the rapid spread of God's Word (2 Thess. 3:1); and for doors to open to the gospel (Col. 4:3).

We should pray in the Holy Spirit. When we reach the end of our prayer rope, he will pray for us (Jude 20; Rom. 8:26-27).

I believe God wants to send a spiritual awakening. We can permit him to do it by having a great outpouring of prayer and dependence upon the Holy Spirit.

I have seen and read some of the touches of his power in this present age. As a college student I was asked to conduct a Vacation Bible School. The pastor was away, but he'd left word that I could preach.

By the third night the balcony was filled, and chairs were placed in the aisles. The chief of police was saved and came bringing his whole family to Christ. Many were saved. Two saloons were closed. The Holy Spirit moved in a most unusual way in that town.

The reason for this outpouring was prayer. Before entering the town, the music director and I stopped our car and asked the Father to give us the town for Christ. We claimed Christ's promise "that if two of you agree on earth about anything that they may ask, it shall be done for them by My Father who is in heaven" (Matt. 18:19).

In 1981 Baptist churches in South Korea reported 180,000 members. In 1982 they had 300,000. The answer: more people are attending prayer meetings than regular worship services. Most of the members go daily to church at 5:00 AM to pray, and then go to work.[2]

In Modesto, California, in 1977, two women committed themselves to faithful prayer for spiritual awakening. In 1982 the awakening came. In two weeks 313 persons professed Christ. Ninety percent of them were adults; 95 percent of them had never been to the church prior to the crusade services.[3]

A church in Euless, Texas, scheduled eight nights of evangelistic services. They continued five more nights. There were 512 professions of faith. Nearly all converts were older young people and adults.[4] There was no special promotion, but fifty to sixty home prayer groups met prior to the crusade.

Stanley Mooneyham, president of World Vision International, says, "Prayer is the one resource immediately available to us all. If more Christians were on their knees praying more Christians would be on their feet witnessing."[5]

8

The Prophetic Scripture Believed

Peter told the early believers, "Brethren, the Scripture had to be fulfilled, which the Holy Spirit foretold" (Acts 1:16). This statement marks the early Christians' belief in the truth and authenticity of the Scriptures. Their belief in and use of the Scriptures had a positive effect on their evangelistic growth.

The word *Scripture* means "writings." The early believers regarded these writings as "holy" and coming from God. They labeled them prophetic Scriptures (2 Pet. 1:20-21).

Scriptures from the Holy Spirit

The early believers stood upon three basic assumptions about the Scriptures.

First, they believed they were given by the Holy Spirit. Peter said the Scripture had to be fulfilled because it was spoken by the Holy Spirit.

Paul spoke of all Scripture as being inspired or "God breathed" (2 Tim. 3:16).

The early Christians believed that the Holy Spirit used men to give God's Word. Peter said that the Holy Spirit spoke through David and that Paul's writings were "God breathed." He equated them with "the rest of the Scriptures" (2 Pet. 3:16).

The Bible declares that "No prophecy was ever made by an act of human will, but men moved by the Holy Spirit spoke from God" (2 Pet. 1:21). This means the prophet did not start the prophecy. He was not a self-starter.[1]

Second, the early Christians believed that Christ was the core of the Scriptures. They learned this from Jesus, who said about the Scriptures, "It is these that bear witness of Me" (John 5:39). He said of Moses, "He wrote of Me" (John 5:46).

Christ emphasized that he was the core of the Scriptures when he said, "All things which are written about Me in the Law of Moses and the Prophets and the Psalms must be fulfilled" (Luke 24:44).

Third, the early Christians believed that Christ was the clue to understanding the Scriptures. The Holy Spirit enlightens the believer to understand Christ and the Scriptures (John 14:26).

Scripture Taught and Preached

The Scriptures play a vital role in evangelistic growth. The new converts devoted "themselves to the apostles' teachings" (Acts 2:42). The Old Testament was taught in the light of the crucifixion, resurrection, and ascension of Christ. Paul taught and preached the Scriptures, "devoting himself completely to the word, . . . testifying . . . that Jesus was the Christ" (Acts 18:5). All this resulted in evangelistic growth. For "many . . . when they heard were believing and being baptized" (Acts 18:8).

The early believers taught and preached the Word of God as authoritative. Peter, upon the authority of the Scriptures, said that someone had to take Judas' place (Acts 1:20-22; Ps. 109:8). Apollos believed in their authority, so "he was mighty in the Scriptures . . . demonstrating by the Scriptures that Jesus was the Christ" (Acts 18:24-25,28).

An authoritative stance on Scripture greatly affects evangelistic growth. Six major denominations lost over 3.5 million members between 1960 and 1979. Harold Lindsell, former editor of *Christianity Today,* said, "It is apparent that declines in both missionary outreach abroad and evangelism at home would be attributed, in part, to the infiltration of theological liberalism."[2]

I heard Lyle E. Shaller, an admired leader in church growth studies, say that flourishing congregations take the Bible seriously. They study it, live it, and pattern their church programs by its principles.

The early believers accepted the Word as the sword of the Holy Spirit (Heb. 4:12; Eph. 6:17). The Word acted as the Spirit's sword at Pentecost, and the people were pierced to the heart (Acts 2:37).

I have seen God's word pierce hearts. Once I asked a woman if she believed the Bible was God's word. She said, "I don't know. Maybe it is. Maybe it isn't." I read her passages about her lost condition and Christ's ability to save. Two days later her heart opened to Christ. Then I asked her about the Bible. She said, "Oh, I believe it's God's word." After she knew the Author, she had no problem believing its authenticity.

They Followed the Scripture

The Holy Spirit says, "Prove yourselves doers of the Word, not merely hearers" (Jas. 1:22). The early believers followed the Word in replacing Judas. They studied it, determined the biblical accuracy of Paul's preaching by it (Acts 17:11), and sought God's approval by it (2 Tim. 2:15).

The serious loss of missionaries among some denominations is traced to a lack of "depth of conviction about basic Christian doctrine—nature of the Gospel, the lostness of mankind apart from Christ".[3]

Those who act on his word, prioritize evangelistic growth (Matt. 28:19; Acts 1:8), and speak God's word boldly (Acts 4:29-31).

Part III
The Performance Principles of Evangelistic Growth

9

The Publicity That Got a Crowd

Did you ever wonder why thousands of people gathered around the apostles on the Day of Pentecost? When the Holy Spirit came upon the believers, God advertised and publicized the happening in a way that brought the people together.

Publicity for the First Evangelistic Service

The Scripture says, "And suddenly there came from heaven a noise like a violent, rushing wind. . . . And when this sound occurred, the multitude came together" (Acts 2:2,6). The sound was like the whirr of a tornado.[1] It wasn't a wind, but it was like a violent wind. The loud sound brought the crowd. The sound came from heaven; God sent it.

God believes in publicity. God the Father and God the Son united in sending God the Holy Spirit. Publicity that will bring crowds to hear the gospel today must be the kind that is inspired by God and will honor him.

God still wants multitudes to hear his word today. God believes in and uses the type of publicity that gets people to hear the gospel. He advertised the birth of his Son with an army of angels, through some shepherds, and by a star.

The news about Christ spread widely and rapidly because of his miracles and his teachings. When the unexplainable begins to happen in the life of a church, word spreads rapidly. The people begin to come.

At Pentecost the believers were filled with the Holy Spirit and were ready to witness when the crowd gathered. A church may be able to attract a crowd, but if it does not give them spiritual food they will soon lose them. When God healed the lame man at the Temple gate, and all the people ran to John and Peter, they preached Jesus to them (Acts 3:7-12). As a result "many of those who had heard the message believed" (Acts 4:4).

Devil's Actions Can Publicize

When Peter and John were brought before a large group of the rulers, Peter took the opportunity to preach Jesus (Acts 4:5-12).

As word spread about a couple being struck dead for lying to the Holy Spirit, God used it to cause multitudes to be saved (Acts 5:1-14).

Paul left the synagogue and went to a house where he could attract more people, and "many . . . when they heard were believing and being baptized" (Acts 18:8).

Publicity in Evangelistic Growth Today

Anything that honors Christ, doesn't contradict the Scriptures, and will get people to hear the gospel is publicity that God can bless.

Publicity that appeals to people will get others to hear the gospel. An outstanding evangelistic friend of mine was won to Christ, as a boy, when a church publicized they were going to give away ice cream. He went for the ice cream, heard the gospel, and received Christ as Savior.

Beautiful music about Christ, amid an unusual setting, attracts thousands of people today. I took the idea of the singing Christmas tree to a large church. Every Christmas thousands of people hear the good news sung, and many are led to Christ.

Churches today can get publicity in newspapers and on radio and television. In Southern California a church is printing a full page of its news in a weekly shopper that is mailed to 60,000 homes. Response has been dramatic. Attendance has doubled in five months. When new people attend, they don't feel like strangers, because they have been reading the church news.[2]

The president of a large trucking firm put a Christian-centered logo on the back of all his vehicles. He receives letters daily from people who are spiritually encouraged by the logo.

In Greece, where there are laws that hinder open preaching, a team of fifty-five people organized to present the gospel at beaches, prison farms, disco centers, and in the main squares of villages and cities. They used contemporary Christian music, a magic show, and preaching. More than 7,000 were attracted to the presentations. Information and New Testaments were given. In Corinth the mayor printed handbills and placed front page advertisements in the city's newspapers. The team fearlessly shared the gospel by aggressive evangelism.[3]

Churches can get those awaiting baptism to invite the unchurched they know to come and see them baptized. This will bring people to hear the gospel.

A child who had made a profession of faith in children's worship later was asking the pastor about being baptized. He said, "Tonight I want to be advertised." The church that will take advantage of advertising to get people to hear the gospel will find avenues of publicity that God will use. Evangelistic growth will happen.

10

The Personal Witnessing by All the Believers

There are two ways to evangelize: personal witnessing and public preaching. The churches in the New Testament majored in personal witnessing. We usually win a few at a time. They won multitudes.

Before Pentecost, Christ told his followers that they would receive power when the Holy Spirit came upon them, and they would be his witnesses (Acts 1:8). At Pentecost "they were all filled with the Holy Spirit and began to speak" (Acts 2:4).

All the Believers Witnessed

In my seminary evangelism class the professor said that the reason 3,000 people came to Christ on the Day of Pentecost was because all of the believers witnessed, probably two or three hours before Peter preached.

We can put the word *all* in Acts 2:4 twice and not misinterpret the verse. They were all filled with the Holy Spirit, and they all began to speak. All believers are included in the command, "You shall be my witnesses" (Acts 1:8).

Christ wants every believer to witness. He told the first disciples to follow him, and he would make them fishers of men. He gave the Great Commission, "Go therefore and make disciples of all the nations" (Matt. 28:19), to all believers. This is a command; it is not optional.

All of the early believers witnessed. The Scripture says that they "went about preaching the word" (Acts 8:4). The Greek word used here for preaching is the same word used for evangelism and gospel. They all went evangelizing or gospelizing. They were not making a formal proclamation. It was the easy speech of evangels. The message was burning and positive. It is no marvel there was evangelistic growth wherever they went.[1]

The early believers had learned personal witnessing from Jesus. Of the recorded decisions to follow Christ, most came from his personal witnessing, not from his public preaching.

All Believers Are Witnesses

A witness is one who can testify from personal experience. Every saved person has had a personal experience with Jesus. He has become a new creation. He has been born again. The Holy Spirit lives in him. From his own experience he can tell others that Jesus saves.

Jesus said that every believer is a witness. On his resurrection day he said, "You are witnesses" (Luke 24:48). On his ascension day he said, "You shall be My witnesses" (Acts 1:8).

The early believers acknowledged that they were Christ's witnesses. Four times they plainly said, "We are witnesses" (Acts 2:32; 3:15; 5:32; 10:39).

You did not choose to be a witness. You were chosen by Christ when he saved you. Becoming a witness is not optional; it is automatic. Witnessing is optional. Every witness does not practice personal witnessing.

I began to do personal witnessing while in high school. I was a pastor and preached publicly for a year without speaking to any on a one-to-one basis about receiving Christ. A pastor, who knew how to witness personally, helped me in a revival crusade. He used the Scriptures to show people how they could receive Christ. Several people were saved in their homes and in other places.

Later, I led a revival crusade. I went throughout the community with my New Testament and presented Christ to people. The Holy Spirit used his Word and me to bring several to Christ.

All Believers Can Witness

Nothing can keep a believer from witnessing if he will yield himself to the Holy Spirit. The Bible says, "For the Spirit that God has given us does not make us timid; instead, his Spirit fills us with power, love, and self-control. Do not be ashamed, then, of witnessing for our Lord" (2 Tim. 1:7-8, GNB).

Every believer needs some teaching in order to be a strong witness. After the new converts were taught, they were witnessing so effectively that "the Lord was adding to their number day by day those who were being saved" (Acts 2:42,47).

Every believer needs the personal joy of helping another to receive Christ.

One year a certain university was only one football game away from being conference champions. As the final game was about to end, their team got the ball. A player who weighed only about 135 pounds, but who was very fast, ran the ball. He darted this way and that until he found an opening. The yards sped under him. He crossed the goal line, winning the game. Players and fans carried him off the field in joyful celebration.

A few weeks later this young man was asked to tell about the happiest experience in his life. He told about the thrill of the game. Then he added, "Now let me tell you about the greatest thrill I've ever had."

On a recent Sunday he had taught a Sunday School class of twelve-year-old girls. As he sat in front of them the Holy Spirit put a thought into his mind. He asked each of them, "Have you ever personally received Christ as your Savior?" One girl said she hadn't, but that she wanted to. He told how he helped her to receive Christ. Then he added, "That is the greatest thrill I have ever had."

Witnessing Is Telling of Christ

Christ said that witnessing is relating four basic truths. We are to tell others of his death, of his resurrection, of their need to repent of their sins, and of Christ's promise of forgiveness. Then Jesus confirmed that these truths are the content, or the body, of the witness when he added, "You are witnesses of these things" (Luke 24:48).

A person witnesses when he gives these four basic truths. His witness is reinforced when he tells about his own saving experience with Christ. A person may argue about the facts of the Bible, but he cannot argue about your personal experience.

Our Lord doesn't ask a witness to be successful. He only asks the witness to be faithful. His Word says that we are "stewards of the mysteries of God" (1 Cor. 4:1). It is a mystery to lost people how a person becomes a child of God, Having a personal knowledge of Christ makes us his ambassadors. He makes his appeal through us (2 Cor. 5:20).

The Lord urges us to be "ready to make a defense to everyone who asks you to give an account for the hope that is in you" (1 Pet. 3:15). We will be ready to witness for Christ if we practice continual spiritual cleansing (1 John 1:9) and continually receive the infilling or control of the Holy Spirit (Eph. 5:18). The Holy Spirit, who also is a witness (Acts 5:32), will empower us.

In churches that are experiencing rapid evangelistic growth today, personal witnessing is the norm instead of the exception. I have a son in a California church that baptizes about 3,000 converts a year. He told me that anyone in that church who doesn't witness is an oddball. I thought, *What a contrast! In some churches a person is an oddball if he does witness for Christ.*

Jesus trained his disciples and sent them out two by two to witness. Today some great programs for training personal witnesses are available. Churches using these training programs are experiencing evangelistic growth.

The power of the Holy Spirit can work in a witness in any situation. During World War II a pastor in the Netherlands was placed in solitary confinement by the Germans. A young parachutist was captured and placed in an adjoining cell. The man learned they could communicate by tapping the Morse code on their walls.

One day the young man tapped, "It is hell to be alone."

The pastor tapped back, "It is heaven to be alone with my Lord."

As the days went by, the pastor tapped out the gospel message to the young man. When the guards came to take the parachutist to his execution, he tapped, "I'm not going out to death. I'm going out to life."

11

The Public Preaching by a Spirit-Filled Man

Whereas personal witnessing is the first facet in New Testament evangelism, public preaching is the second. There are two principal words that are translated "preach." One means to testify to the good news on a personal basis, such as person to person. The other word means to speak as a herald to a crowd.

Both facets of evangelism were used in evangelistic growth. All the believers personally witnessed (Acts 2:4), and Peter spoke as a herald (Acts 2:14). A herald speaks with urgency about an emergency. He speaks with authority that calls for action.

The word for preach that means to herald the gospel comes from the background of the Greek city-states. Each city had a town crier or herald. He received news the citizens needed to know; then he went down the streets crying out this news. Upon hearing the news the citizens had to take action accordingly.

Both words for preach are used to describe Christ's speaking. He said he must preach, or announce, the good news of the kingdom (Luke 4:43). He also preached, or proclaimed, as a herald (Matt. 9:35).

Both words described the preaching of the early believers. When they preached to people on a more personal basis, the word used meant that they were "gospelizing" or "evangelizing" (Acts 5:42; 8:4).

When Philip preached to multitudes, he spoke as a herald (Acts 8:5-6). When he preached to one man he spoke as one announcing good news to another (Acts 8:35).

Paul used both words to describe his preaching. He said that Christ sent him "to preach [evangelize] the gospel." He also said that "God was well-pleased through the foolishness of the message preached [heralded] to save those who believe" (1 Cor. 1:17,21).

Spirit-Filled Preaching

Peter had just been filled with the Holy Spirit when he stood up to speak (Acts 2:4). A few days later the Scripture says of him, "Then Peter, filled with the Holy Spirit, said to them . . . " (Acts 4:8).

Look at some of the characteristics of Peter's preaching that escalated evangelistic growth.

Peter preached boldly. He stood up, and spoke up (Acts 2:14). He was no longer the coward as when he denied Jesus. Christ assured him of forgiveness by going to him personally after his resurrection (Luke 24:34; 1 Cor. 15:5). Christ had also recommissioned him (John 21:15-19). Now, filled with the Holy Spirit, Peter preached with great power.

His boldness showed when he refuted the mockers outright (Acts 2:15). His preaching was with fervency and urgency.

Personal Preaching

Peter's preaching was personal. The people had no doubt as to whom he was preaching. He said *you* twelve times in the brief section of the sermon that is recorded (Acts 2:14-39).

Paul also used the pronoun *you* in his preaching. He said, "You who fear God, listen: . . . we preach to you the good news. . . . Therefore let it be known to you, brethren, that through Him forgiveness of sins is proclaimed to you" (Acts 13:16,32,38).

Jesus was a personal preacher. He said to a crowd, "You are from below, . . . you are of this world; . . . you shall die in your sins" (John 8:23-24).

In spiritual awakenings throughout history, preaching is marked by the direct personal appeal. Jonathan Edwards' preaching was so powerful and personal that men cried out in emotion during the sermons. George Whitfield and John Wesley preached so personally and boldly that throngs of people stood in the open with rapt attention.

Preaching today that the Holy Spirit can use to bring about evangelistic growth from the masses must be personal in its delivery and appeal. Billy Graham is the prime example.

Biblical Preaching

Peter's preaching was authoritative. He took his stand upon the Word of God. Using Joel, he showed that God had promised the coming of the Holy Spirit (Acts 2:16-21). He used two passages from Psalms to prove the resurrection of Christ (Acts 2:25-28,34-35).

Billy Graham says that when he decided to stand on the Word of God he became authoritative in his preaching. In his sermons he has often said, "The Bible says . . . "

Paul's preaching was biblical. The Scripture says he was preaching the "word of the Lord" (Acts 15:35). He instructed others to "preach the word" (2 Tim. 4:2).

We who desire evangelistic growth today must be biblical preachers. The Holy Spirit will use the Word to pierce hearts. It is his sword (Acts 2:37; Eph. 6:17).

Christ-Centered Preaching

Peter's preaching was Christ centered. Only Christ-centered preaching will be utilized by the Holy Spirit. He came to bear witness to and to glorify Christ (John 15:26; 16:14). Peter's message was not about psychology, child care, national defense, or race relations. It was about Christ, who could correct all things.

Peter said that Christ proved himself as the Messiah in the following ways:

First, Jesus proved himself by his works. He declared that God had accredited him "with miracles and wonders and signs" (Acts 2:23).

Second, Jesus proved himself as the Messiah by dying in the will of God. They had nailed him to the cross, but this was in the "predetermined plan and foreknowledge of God" (Acts 2:23).

Third, Peter preached that Jesus proved himself as the Messiah by his resurrection (Acts 2:24-32). Proclamation of the death and resurrection of Christ is gospel preaching.

Fourth, Peter said that Jesus proved himself as the Messiah by his exaltation at the right hand of God (Acts 2:33a).

Fifth, Peter proclaimed that Jesus proved himself to be the Messiah by cooperating with the Father in sending the Holy Spirit (Acts 2:33b).

Sixth, Peter declared that Jesus was the Messiah because God had made him both Lord and Christ (Acts 2:36).

Decision-Directed Preaching

Peter preached for decisions (Acts 2:38). This is one of the vital marks of evangelistic preaching. It gives purpose to the preaching.

One of Spurgeon's students came to him disturbed that few people were being saved under his preaching. Spurgeon asked him, "You don't expect someone to be saved every time you preach do you?" The student replied that he did not. Then Spurgeon said, "That's why you don't have them."

Bishop Hudson of London spoke of decision-directed preaching as follows: "The first purpose of evangelism is to seek and save those who are lost. . . . We must win from the individual that decision on which his salvation now depends."[1]

Preaching is not evangelistic if it isn't decision directed. Facts of the message may be there, but it will be dry and dusty. There must be an urgency in preaching. The love of God and the nature of lost people demand it.

Christ called people to decision. The early believers followed his example. Today let's permit the urgency of the Holy Spirit to fall upon us. Let's preach for decisions for Christ. Evangelistic growth will come!

12

The Piercing of the Lost by the Holy Spirit

The Holy Spirit has a ministry with lost people. Jesus said the Holy Spirit would "convict the world concerning sin, and righteousness, and judgment" (John 16:8).

The Holy Spirit convicted people on the Day of Pentecost. After hearing the witness of the 120 and the preaching of Peter, "they were pierced in the heart" (Acts 2:37). The word *pierce* is a strong word. It's a picture of a dueler being run straight through by a blade. It means the crowd was deeply troubled or smitten in conscience. They were hopelessly wounded in the soul. Since Jesus was actually the appointed Messiah, Peter said they had rejected their only hope. As a result they were in deep despair. They showed their despair by crying out, "What shall we do?" (Acts 2:37).[1]

Only the Holy Spirit Can Pierce Hearts

The work of piercing hearts is unique to the Holy Spirit. The sound of a mighty wind, tongues of fire, and languages spoken did not produce the piercing.

The use of psychology doesn't pierce hearts. Man can manipulate the mind, but only the Holy Spirit can pierce the heart. Two things must occur in the life of a lost person which only the Holy Spirit can cause.

First, only the Holy Spirit can show Jesus to a person.

The Holy Spirit never exalts himself; he always exalts Jesus (John 15:26). Jesus said of the Holy Spirit, "He shall glorify Me" (John 16:14). *Glorify* means to reveal his true nature. The Holy Spirit unveils Christ to minds that have been blinded by Satan.

Second, only the Holy Spirit can show lost people their lostness. When the Pentecost crowd had a clear understanding of Jesus, they became deeply troubled about themselves. They were pierced to the heart.

A Pierced Heart Is Essential for Salvation

No one can be saved until the Holy Spirit speaks to him. Jesus said, "No one can come to Me, unless the Father who sent Me draws him" (John 6:44). The Holy Spirit always takes the initiative. When lost people hear the good news about Christ, the Holy Spirit uses the message to pierce their hearts.

For the lost person to respond to Christ, he must have a felt need. It is the Holy Spirit who brings this felt need for Christ. Apart from the work of the Holy Spirit a lost person cannot be saved.

The people to whom Peter preached on the Day of Pentecost were already religiously oriented and conformed to certain doctrines and beliefs. It was not until they were pierced through the heart that they felt a need for Christ. As long as a lost person thinks he's all right spiritually, apart from Christ, he won't have a felt need for spiritual help. It is the Holy Spirit who brings him to the felt need and points him to Christ.

Piercing Instruments

The instruments used by the Holy Spirit to bring a lost person to his felt need for Christ are twofold.

First, he uses the word or message about Christ. The

people at Pentecost were pierced to their hearts "when they heard this" (Acts 2:37). It was the message about Jesus that the Holy Spirit used to awaken the people to a felt need for Christ. Notice the content of the message.

They had proof that Jesus was of God because of the signs and miracles which he did. His death did not come about by an accumulation of circumstances but was predetermined in the plan of God. However, they had acted to bring about his death. God had raised him and exalted him to his right hand of power and authority. This Jesus, whom they had crucified, was now Messiah and Lord.

From the message, the people saw they had a wrong relationship with Christ. Their past attitudes and actions toward the Messiah were wrong. They saw themselves in a spiritually precarious position: "What shall we do?" (Acts 2:37).

The second instrument of the Holy Spirit, used to pierce hearts, was the person who presented the message. The Scripture asks, "How shall they hear without a preacher?" (Rom. 10:14). The Holy Spirit uses those who preach the message convincingly and authoritatively. Paul spoke out of his personal experience with Christ. He had become an ambassador for Christ. God made his appeal through him (2 Cor. 5:20).

It is awesome to observe a lost person when the Holy Spirit uses the message and the messenger to pierce his heart. I was having a casual conversation with a man when the Holy Spirit turned our talk to the things of Christ. His face drained of color. He began to tremble, and expressed his felt need for Christ. When he asked Christ to become his Lord and Savior, he became very calm. He expressed a sense of inner joy and peace. He told other members of his family of his decision for Christ and made his public stand for Christ through baptism.

Piercing Occurs in Three Areas

Christ said the Holy Spirit would convict the world in three areas: sin, righteousness, and judgment (John 16:8). The word *convict* means to bring to light, or expose, and to refute with a view to correction.

First, the Holy Spirit exposes a person's sin. He refutes his claim of innocence or self-righteousness with a view of correcting him if he will surrender himself to Christ in repentance and faith.[2]

Jesus explained the connection of sin by saying, "Concerning sin, because they do not believe in Me" (John 16:9). The Holy Spirit shows the blackness and the grossness of the sin of unbelief with respect to Jesus Christ.

Peter told the crowd at Pentecost, "you" nailed him to the cross. The word *you* is emphatic. They had rejected and crucified the one who was now the Lord of glory (Acts 2:36-37). Subsequently, they were now numbered among the crucifiers (Heb. 6:6).

Second, the Holy Spirit convinces or pierces in the realm of righteousness. Jesus explained this by saying, "Concerning righteousness, because I go to the Father" (John 16:10). Jesus went to the Father by the cross and resurrection. By these acts he makes it possible for one to come under the righteousness of God.

The Holy Spirit shows the lost person he has no righteousness, but the lost person may receive God's righteousness by receiving Christ.

Third, the Holy Spirit convicts in the area of judgment. Jesus explained this by saying, "Because the ruler of this world has been judged" (John 16:11). The word *judged* means a full, complete judgment. Through Christ, God rendered final judgment on Satan. This judgment falls upon all who choose to follow him. When one commits himself to Christ, he or she is no longer condemned (John 3:18).

The crowd at Pentecost felt this judgment. The Holy Spirit showed them that the answer to their predicament was to turn away from their sins. Then Christ, in his authority, could give them forgiveness and the gift of the Holy Spirit. They were to register their decision for accepting the person of Jesus as the Messiah through baptism.

Conversion comes from a deep-felt need for Christ, caused by the Holy Spirit, through the message and messenger of Christ. People are saved and evangelistic growth takes place under the convincing power of the Holy Spirit.

13

The Prerequisite Requirement for Salvation

Repentance is essential for salvation. It must be emphasized to have evangelistic growth.

When some in the Pentecost crowd came to see that they were wrong in their relation to the risen Messiah, they asked what they had to do. They were told to repent (Acts 2:38). This attitude and act would reshape the totality of their lives and their destiny.

There are two words for repent in the New Testament. One word points toward self. The other points toward God. The Scripture says that Judas repented (Matt. 27:3, KJV). The word used means he felt sorry for himself. His primary concern was for his problem and predicament.

The other word used for repentance (Acts 2:38) means a godly sorrow. The person is primarily concerned about what sin has done to his relationship with God. He also is concerned about what he can do to set this relationship right.[1]

Repentance also involves change. It means a change of mind that leads to a change of conduct.

Peter told the Pentecost crowd that their attitude toward the Messiah had been wrong. They must have a change at the core of their nature, so they would never be the same again.

The word *repent* used by Peter is in the imperative. It is something they must do. Only this would make them right with the Messiah and with life itself.

To have evangelistic growth, people must be called upon to change their minds and their attitudes concerning Jesus as Messiah, in view of removing their sins. Repentance does not involve the mere fact of personal salvation but also the righting of one's life.[2] People must turn right about, and do it now. The Jesus they had crucified they must now crown as Lord. They must make a radical and complete change of their lives.[3] Repentance includes turning from a "perverse generation" (Acts 2:40).

Repentance is a turning from self and known sin. If one is in love with himself and the delights of sin, he has not repented. The love of God is not in him (1 John 2:15). He is an enemy of God (Jas. 4:4). The principle and power of sin is broken when one repents.

Jesus and Repentance

Jesus connected repentance with faith. He said, "Repent and believe in the gospel" (Mark 1:15). Jesus taught that we have a choice: repent or perish. He said that repentance is so important, heaven takes notice (Luke 15:7).

Jesus taught the reason people go to hell is because they don't repent (Luke 16:30-31). He taught the necessity of repentance to have forgiveness of sins. He made this a part of the gospel witness (Luke 24:46-48).

Early Believers and Repentance

When Peter called for repentance, he was preaching what Jesus had taught. He preached that people were personally related to the death of Christ, but God had raised him; therefore, they must repent. Their sins would be wiped away (Acts 3:14-19). This preaching of repentance was followed by great evangelistic growth. The number of men reached five thousand (Acts 4:4).

When Peter and the apostles were called before the council, the Jewish leaders were told that Jesus as the Messiah could "grant repentance to Israel, and forgiveness of sins" (Acts 5:31).

As the gospel spread across the Roman Empire the message of repentance was preached. Paul declared at Athens that God had called on all men everywhere to repent because he had fixed a day in which he would judge the world by Jesus (Acts 17:30-31). Paul summarized his message as "repentance toward God and faith in our Lord Jesus Christ" (Acts 20:21). When he stood before a king he said he had always preached that men "should repent and turn to God, performing deeds appropriate to repentance" (Acts 26:20).

Repentance and Evangelistic Growth Today

Peter declared three things about repentance that determines evangelistic growth.

First, each person must repent. Each one was to demonstrate his repentance by baptism. In our day we hear talk about society being guilty. The Bible teaches that each person is guilty and must repent toward God and put his faith in Christ. Society is changed when people are changed. When a person repents, he changes his mental attitudes and conduct and will help change society about him.[4]

Second, Peter preached that repentance was necessary for forgiveness of sins. People need to know that forgiveness does not come by church membership, by baptism, or by reformation. It comes by repentance: getting right with God by dethroning self and enthroning Christ.

Third, Peter taught that repentance would bring from Jesus the gift of the Holy Spirit in the life of the believer. This is the answer to those who say, "I am too weak to live the Christian life." The Holy Spirit becomes their enabler.

The call for repentance is a call for response. Jesus said that Nineveh responded in repentance at the preaching of Jonah. Christ is greater than Jonah. People today are called upon to repent in the light of who Jesus is and their relation to him (Matt. 12:41).

On the Day of Pentecost people responded to the call of repentance; "those who had received his word were baptized" (Acts 2:41). Human nature and human need remain the same. The gospel of Christ remains the same. Today we can know that persons will respond to the call of repentance by the power of the Holy Spirit. Evangelistic growth will result.

Without the call to repentance there can be no evangelistic growth. One cannot turn to God until one turns away from one's sins. The Lord is "not wishing for any to perish but for all to come for repentance" (2 Pet. 3:9). The call to repentance must be boldly sounded. When this occurs, some will believe (Acts 17:30-34). Evangelistic growth will happen.

14

The Persuasion of the Lost

One day in chapel at the Southern Baptist Theological Seminary, the president, Ellis Fuller, told this story. While he was pastor in Atlanta, the secretary of a men's Bible class had heard him preach every Sunday. However, he had not received Christ. Each Sunday, after hearing the sermon, he went away as if nothing had occurred. Dr. Fuller said this began to greatly bother him. A man was hearing him preach every Sunday, but the gospel didn't seem to affect hm.

One Saturday he went to talk to the man. He stopped his car in front of the house, blew the horn, and signaled for the man to come and sit with him. When the man had gotten in the front seat, Dr. Fuller said he turned to him and said, "I'm not going to mince words with you. I think a great deal of you. The men at our church regard you highly. That's why they made you secretary of their Bible class. You are a fine person in many ways. But, I want you to know, sir, you are just as lost as any person who as ever lived. If you die like you are, you are going to go straight to hell. You have no hope, whatsoever, in Jesus Christ."

The man turned, reach for the car door, opened it, got out, slammed it behind him, walked across the lawn, and closed his door. Reluctantly, Dr. Fuller turned his car toward home, saying to himself, "Well, I guess I blew that one."

The next morning when the man had dressed for church his wife called "Honey, breakfast is ready." He walked down the hall and turned the corner into the breakfast nook. Then he stopped. There was something different about the table. In a moment he made it out. The plates were upside down. His wife never set the table that way.

As he was seated he turned his plate over. Then he saw the note. It was in his wife's handwriting. "Dear John, I would have said this to you personally, but I knew I would have started crying and not been able to finish. John, I love you so much I feel I shall die if you don't receive Christ. He means so much to me. I just don't know what I will do if you don't receive him also."

He looked up from the note, across the corner of the table, into his wife's eyes that were streaming with tears. In a moment he said, "Honey, if Jesus is that real to you, he must certainly be real. Will you pray with me right now, as I ask God to forgive me and make me his child too?"

Dr. Fuller said when he preached that Sunday and gave the invitation, the man was the first one to the altar. He said, "Because I have a wife who cares and because she wouldn't give up on me, I have received Christ as my Savior. I want to follow him in baptism in this church."

She persuaded her husband. Persuasion can be gentle. It also may be bombastic. This is probably the way Peter's was on the Day of the Pentecost. He did something that was different from regular preaching. "He solemnly testified and kept on exhorting them" (Acts 2:40). There was a note of great urgency in his words.

Peter was persuading the people. Paul believed in persuading people. He said, "Knowing the fear of the Lord, we persuade men" (2 Cor. 5:11). This is needed in preaching and witnessing today.

When Peter "testified" to the people, he was not subdued. He was excited! The word *testify* means to present a solemn witness. He was witnessing to evoke a response to Christ.

The Greek word for "exhort" means to call to oneself. Peter was asking the people to come over to his side, over to Christ's side. It was a call to decision, a call to turn from the crowd, and a call to turn to Christ through repentance. He didn't give a brief call. He kept on exhorting them.

The ability to exhort seems to be a gift from the Lord (Rom. 12:8). The word described the preaching of John the Baptist (Luke 3:18).

Did you know that years ago churches had people who were called exhorters? George Truett, pastor at First Baptist in Dallas for years, told that soon after he was saved his pastor called upon him to exhort. There were people without Christ in the service, but no one was responding to the invitation. Dr. Truett said that even though he was timid, he forgot himself.

He not only exhorted in front of the congregation, he began to go down the left aisle. Looking down each row, he pointed to men and women by name saying to them, "John, Mary, you know you need Christ. Come to him tonight. Go to the altar and ask him to save you."

He circled the back of the church. Then he came down the right aisle, speaking to individuals, urging them, and exhorting them. Soon the altar was filled with adults asking the Lord for salvation. Truett said he suddenly came to himself, realized where he was, and very timidly went to his seat. God had used him as an exhorter.

Basis for Persuasion

The word *persuade* means to move and to entice for a decision. There is a biblical basis for persuading people concerning Christ and salvation. Most of us are timid by nature. We shrink at the thought of trying to persuade people, especially about the Lord. The Holy Spirit can empower us and overcome our timidity. Every child of God can and should be a persuader. God's preachers, especially, need to be persuaders.

The "fear of the Lord" is a biblical basis for persuading people. Since we have been assigned the task and opportunity of witnessing, the Scripture seems to indicate we will give an account of the same at the judgment. It was in this context Paul said he tried to persuade men (2 Cor. 5:11). Those who opposed his preaching complimented him when they said, "This man persuades men to worship God" (Acts 18:13). To help people to receive Christ, "he was reasoning in the synagogue every Sabbath and trying to persuade Jews and Greeks" (Acts 18:4). How much persuading do you and I do to help people to the Savior?

A description of Paul's ministry is one of continued reasoning and persuading. Everywhere he went he was persuading people (Acts 19:8,26). A king acknowledged Paul tried to persuade him to become a Christian (Acts 26:28). Even in Paul's confinement in Rome, he was still about the same business of persuading. Large numbers came to him and he solemnly testified, trying to persuade them concerning Jesus. Some were persuaded (Acts 28:23-24).

Human nature demands that Christians be persuaders. By nature human beings do not come toward God. They go away from him. By nature people are separated from God. By nature they are in danger (Eph. 2:1-3; Col. 2:13).

It is our nature to procrastinate. Roy Fish says that by nature man is spiritually lethargic. He needs encouragement to respond to the gospel offer.[1] Man doesn't do right just because he knows right. He must be persuaded to decision.

People also live in a social structure that pulls them away from God. Christ said there are many who walk the broad road that leads to destruction. If people go with society, they go downward. Leighton Ford says that people living in this kind of society will not be won by a "cool" philosophy. The fire and flame of "a passion for souls" always stands in need of being rekindled.[2]

The gospel is a basis for persuading people to accept Christ. The very nature of the message compels us to appeal for response. The command to repentance, joined with the gospel, calls us to persuasion. The crucified, risen Lord demands response (Luke 24:46-47; Acts 3:19).

Art of Persuasion

There is no wrong way to persuade a person to Christ. There are some ways that may be better than others.

Persuasion is psychologically sound. There are those who are afraid that people's personalities will be overrun and they will be overpersuaded. This is a danger, but there is much more danger in leaving people alone. No one is ever saved until the Holy Spirit convicts them. The Holy Spirit uses the message of Christ and the messengers of Christ to convince people of their need for Christ.

Impression without expression brings depression. People who have been told of the Savior need to be called to make a positive response. Billy Graham says that his invitation to people to "come forward" has been studied by psychologists and psychiatrists. Most of them say it is psychologically good for people to be asked to respond to important issues that they face.

The art of persuasion is more caught than taught. One must have compassion. Jesus wept over a lost city.

Persuasion springs from theological beliefs. The lost condition and peril of one without Christ must be believed. The urgency and shortness of the time must be considered.

Grady Cothen says there are not enough preachers and missionaries "called" by God to do the work that it will take to bring multitudes of people to Christ. Persuading men to Christ must become the business of all who believe in Christ.[3]

Urgency of Persuasion

The importance of a life calls for urgent persuasion. Jesus came that one's life could be full, abundant, and complete (John 10:10). A person never has this kind of life until he knows Christ personally.

Lives get caught up in society and take a downward plunge. Peter exhorted the people, "Be saved from this perverse generation!" (Acts 2:40). A perverse people is a crooked people. It's people who are wrong with God. People must be persuaded to take a stand against their peers. Their peers have frustrated, tangled, and unhappy lives. They must come to Christ to have peace, meaning, and joy in life. A life lived without Christ is a lost life. It is an empty life. For the sake of a person's life now, one needs to be persuaded to Jesus.

We have the ministry of helping people to get right with God. We have the message to help people get right with God. We are the messengers to help people get right with God. We need to be about the business of persuading (2 Cor. 5:18-20).

The urgency of persuading people to Christ is described in the Bible in words that have a fervency about them. *Entreating* is a word of urgency. Christ wants to entreat others through us. The only plan Christ has for entreating others is through us.

The word *beg* carries urgency. We are to beg people, on behalf of Christ, to get right with God. He wants to make his appeal through us. How long has it been since you've begged one to receive Christ?

The word *urge* is a descriptive word for persuasion. We are instructed to urge people not to accept God's grace in vain. It was all in vain that God put his Son on the cross for the person who does not receive him (2 Cor. 5:20; 6:1).

The uncertainty of life and the lost person's danger of dying without Christ adds urgency to the business of persuasion. Twice, God says that "now" is the time to be saved (2 Cor. 6:2).

A lost person also is under danger of becoming hardened by the deceitfulness of sin (Heb. 3:13). He is in danger of quenching the call of the Holy Spirit till he may no longer sense the Lord drawing him (1 Thess. 5:19).

The Holy Spirit, three times in quick succession, gives the urgent call for persons to be persuaded today. He even says that God has set "a certain day" for people to make decisions. That day is "today" (Heb. 3:7-8,15; 4:7). A person never knows when he will have his last opportunity to be persuaded. We never know when we will have our last opportunity to persuade.

D. L. Moody told a Chicago crowd to go home and think about their need to receive Christ and to come back the next night. That crowd never met again. Many were lost in the great Chicago fire that very night. Moody declared he would never preach again without trying to persuade people to the Savior.

An invitation for people to receive Christ should become a part of the sermon. Peter led right into his invitation. The sermon was decision directed. He called for people to respond; he expected them to respond; they did respond.

When we witness, the Holy Spirit also witnesses (Acts 5:32). He will always stir up hearts when we deliver the message persuasively.

Not only the growth of the church makes persuasion imperative, but the very future of the church gives urgency to persuasion. Before evangelistic growth can be a productive program, it must be a passion in the heart. Emil Brunner is reported to have said, "The church exists by mission as fire exists by burning." It's mission must be to bring people to the Savior. The fire of God needs to burn in our persuasion.

A man arose at a meeting and prayed, "Lord, if any spark of revival has been lit in this meeting, we pray that you will water that spark!" Just as he prayed incorrectly, we sometimes labor and preach incorrectly. We fail to call people by urgent persuasion.

The urgency of persuasion was brought vividly to my attention. I read the newspaper headlines about a school blowing up in New London, Texas. Later I heard Marshall Craig, a pastor in Fort Worth, say he had just been in revival services in New London. One night, just before service time, a deacon came to the church office, stating that he wanted to tell him something that might help him appeal with urgency for people to receive Christ that very night.

He reached for his wallet and pulled out a picture. Dr. Craig said it looked like a boy of about nine to twelve years of age. As he returned the picture, he noticed the tears on the deacon's face. He related to Dr. Craig how their little boy had been in the school that had blown up. That fateful day as he was getting ready for school, he told his dad and mother that if anything should happen to him that day they were not to worry about him, because he had received Christ. The man related how they stood at the front door and told him good-bye. He looked into their faces and for the second time he reminded them not to worry about him should something occur, because he knew the Lord.

He said they stood and watched him go down their sidewalk and turn onto the main sidewalk. Then he stopped and for the third time he said, "Now remember, if anything happens today, don't worry about me. I have received Christ as my Savior." He said the boy went on to school. He and his wife talked about why he would say this. He'd never said anything like that before. The clock moved along. It became noon. They finally forgot about what their son had said. And then, just before time for school to be out, they heard the terrible explosion. They rushed to the school with other frantic parents. There wasn't much they could do at first. The fire was so hot.

(When I told this story in a church, a man said, "I was in that school. I'm one of the few that got out alive. The explosion was so terrific, some parents, who had driven up out front for their children, were also killed.")

The father related how, after the fire had died down, he and other men of the city began to probe the debris.

As he pushed away some blackened bricks and some charred timbers, he saw a leg protruding. He said, "I reached down and clasped that leg, and I pulled out the body of my own little boy. Then I seemed to hear him say, 'Remember, if anything happens to me today, don't you worry about me, because I have received Christ.' "

15

The Public Profession by Baptism

When Christ called people to follow him, he called them to open commitment. He said, "Every one therefore who shall confess Me before men, I will also confess him before My Father who is in heaven" (Matt. 10:32).

John the Baptist called people to repentance and to open confession of their sins. They showed their repentance by public baptism (Matt. 3:1-6).

The Jews had a form of baptism called "washing" which symbolized the act of ceremonial cleansing (Heb. 9:10). When a Gentile accepted the Jewish faith, he went through proselyte baptism. It was an open declaration of that faith.[1]

When John began to baptize, he added a new dimension to the symbol. He didn't just have the act, he had the meaning of the act (Acts 19:3). His baptism was not a rite of ceremonial cleansing. It symbolized the person's repentance and his willingness to become a part of the Kingdom that was at hand.

As Christ's disciples began to baptize, baptism took on still another meaning (John 4:1-2). This baptism not only pointed to the Kingdom, it also pointed to the King.

Christ declared himself openly as the Son of God through public baptism. The Scripture says, "When all the people were baptized, . . . Jesus also was baptized" (Luke 3:21). At the Jordan River, John identified Jesus openly as the Savior (John 1:29). The Father and the Holy Spirit also identified Jesus openly at his baptism (Matt. 3:16-17).

As Peter completed his sermon on the Day of Pentecost, he called upon those who repented to register their decisions openly through baptism (Acts 2:38). Throughout New Testament history, those who received Christ as their Messiah were expected to be baptized. It was usually an immediate act after their commitment to Christ (Acts 2:41; 8:12,35-38; 16:31-33).

Believer's Baptism

Christ taught that baptism was for those that had become disciples (Matt. 28:19). Peter placed baptism after repentance. Those baptized had received the message about Jesus and the necessity of repentance to have forgiveness (Acts 2:36-41).

As the gospel spread beyond Jerusalem, only those who professed to believe the good news were baptized. When people "believed Philip, preaching the good news . . . they were being baptized" (Acts 8:12). Philip witnessed to the Ethiopian, taking the Scriptures and "preached [evangelized] Jesus to him" (Acts 8:35). After the man was evangelized, he immediately asked for baptism.

A whole household was baptized immediately after hearing the message of the Lord. The Scripture is careful to note that joy came from believing and not from baptism (Acts 16:32-34). The word *believe* is a perfect participle. It's not accepting facts about Jesus. It's personally committing oneself to him and staying committed to him. It was after this commitment that people were baptized in the early churches. In Greece, the Scripture says, "Many of the Corinthians when they heard were believing and being baptized" (Acts 18:8).

The weight of the Scripture shows that it was believers who were baptized. They had received the gift of the Holy Spirit prior to their baptism (Acts 10:47).

The early believers' open stand through baptism greatly influenced evangelistic growth. Their allegiance to the Messiah was shown openly and every baptism symbolized his resurrection. Baptism is not an option for believers. It is included in Christ's Great Commission for all believers (Matt. 28:19).

Symbol of Christ's Resurrection

Thayer, in his Greek-English lexicon, shows at least five different times that the word *baptism* means to immerse.[2] Immersion gives evangelistic meaning to baptism.

When Jesus was buried and raised in baptism in the Jordan River, he said it was "to fulfill all righteousness" (Matt. 3:15). He was announcing at the beginning of his ministry the purpose of his coming. In order to make sinners righteous, he was going to become sin for them through his death. He would prove his victory over sin by being raised from the dead. Burial and resurrection by baptism in the Jordan was a foretaste and a picture of his coming burial and resurrection.

The gospel is the good news about the death and resurrection of Jesus (1 Cor. 15:1-4). When a believer was buried and raised in baptism, he was symbolizing to all who saw and heard that he had a Savior who died for his sins and had been raised victoriously. Peter declared that the meaning of the act of baptism related to the resurrection of Christ (1 Pet. 3:21).[3]

The only form of baptism in the early church was by immersion. The symbol of the resurrected Savior was continually portrayed before the lost world.

Symbol of Christian's Spiritual Resurrection

Three times the Scriptures speak of baptism showing not only the resurrection of Christ but also the spiritual resurrection of the believer. He once was dead in sin. Now he is alive in Christ. His baptism symbolizes his new position in Christ.

First, baptism served as a badge, or a uniform, to show that a person had entered into the service of the risen Christ. The Scripture says, "For all of you who are baptized into Christ have clothed yourselves with Christ" (Gal. 3:27). *Clothed* does not mean that one enters into Christ and is saved by baptism. It means just the opposite. We are justified by faith in Christ. Baptism is the public profession and pledge to Christ. It is like a soldier putting on a uniform and making a sacred oath of fidelity.[4]

Second, the Scripture presents baptism as the matchless preacher of the new life the believer has in Christ. It is a picture of our past condition, that of being dead in sin. It is a picture of our present condition, that of being alive in Christ. It is also a prophecy of the future, that we shall be raised by Christ.

Baptism does not bring the reality of the new life. It is the symbol and picture of the reality (Rom. 6:1-6).[5] Baptism is the public proclamation of one's inward spiritual relation to Christ. This proclamation brings evangelistic results.

Third, baptism symbolizes that God, who had the "energy" to raise Jesus from the dead, had also raised us up with him through faith.[6] It symbolizes that we, who were dead in our transgressions, have been made alive with Christ and have been forgiven of our transgressions. Baptism is a vivid, symbolic picture of our burial with Christ and resurrection to newness of life in him (Col. 2:13).

When a church makes baptism an end instead of a symbol, history proves that it will eventually cease to have evangelistic growth. The church will fill up with lost people who are depending upon baptism for their salvation.

The church is not a saving institution. It is an institution of the saved. The church is not a redeeming organization. It is an organism of redeemed persons. The business of the church is not to save people but to point people to Jesus Christ who saves them. The believer through baptism symbolically points to his living Savior and his new life in him.

Churches that preach Christ for salvation, symbolize Christ's burial and resurrection through baptism, and follow the Spirit's leading will experience evangelistic growth.

16

The Preserving
of the New Believers

What would you and your church do with 3,000 new converts? This was the opportunity faced by 120 believers immediately following the Day of Pentecost. Some church leaders (who usually aren't doing much about evangelistic growth) accuse growing churches of "dipping and dropping" the converts. Some of this accusation may be true.

A Want-to to Learn

The new converts seemed to have an insatiable desire to learn and to grow spiritually. The Bible says, "They were continually devoting themselves to the apostles' teaching" (Acts 2:42). One of the marks of conversion is the desire to do the will of Christ. He said, "If you love Me, you will keep My commandments" (John 14:15).

In some ways Christian growth is more caught than taught. It is more experience than it is content. Something that is dead cannot grow. It is the born-again believer who has the thirst to grow.

A Willingness to Teach

The apostles were willing to teach the new converts. They were obedient to Christ who said to teach "them to observe all that I have commanded you" (Matt. 28:20).

The apostles' willingness to teach was aided by the Holy Spirit. He was teaching them and bringing to their remembrance the things that Christ had taught them (John 14:26).

The convert is never fully evangelized until he becomes an evangelist. The first converts were so thoroughly taught and filled with the Holy Spirit that, when they were thrust from the city, they "went about preaching the word" (Acts 8:4). The word here for preaching is the word *evangelizing*.

The apostles, no doubt, taught the new converts much that we find in the four Gospels. We can be certain the apostles used the Old Testament in their teaching. Peter used it when he preached on the Day of Pentecost (Acts 2:16-21,25-28,34-35).

Jesus had made the Old Testament come alive to them after his resurrection. He had shown the apostles from the Scripture that he was the core of the Old Testament. Through the Holy Spirit Christ was the clue to their understanding it (Luke 24:44-48).

The apostles surely did not neglect to teach the new converts of the one command that Jesus gave in the Great Commission, and the last command that he gave before he ascended (Matt. 28:19; Acts 1:8). They were taught to witness. The 120 couldn't take the gospel to the whole world. They had to multiply their witness. One of the shackles of evangelistic growth in churches is that new converts are not taught what the gospel really is and what it means to witness for Christ. As the new converts would be crisscrossing the Roman Empire, they needed to have hidden in their hearts what Christ had taught. These truths would reinforce their personal testimony. The Holy Spirit would use their testimony, with the body of truth, and cause the lost listeners to be pierced to the heart (Acts 2:37).

Essentials for Preserving New Converts

A convert is best preserved when he learns to give himself away. Christ taught that those who gave their lives away in service to him would find real life.

First, the apostles made the first church a teaching church. The converts were baptized immediately and then taught. Christ placed this order in his Great Commission.

Second, the apostles helped the new converts to engage in fellowship with other believers. The word means that they became partners or sharers in common interests. It also involves participation or communion (1 Cor. 10:16). Fellowship involves a togetherness. When English Commander Nelson was asked to describe how he had won a great victory he replied, "I commanded a band of brothers."

The Scripture calls for fellowship. "Let us consider how to stimulate one another to love and good deeds, not forsaking our own assembling together, as is the habit of some, but encouraging one another; and all the more, as you see the day drawing near" (Heb. 10:24-25). Christians cannot stay close to the Lord if they don't stay close to fellow believers. When you remove a red hot coal from a fireplace, it soon becomes cold. This is somewhat the picture of the believer who removes himself from the fellowship of other believers.

Satan hates the fellowship of believers. He tried to destroy it by liars and murmurers in the church (Acts 5:1-10; 6:1-6).

The Scripture teaches of our having fellowship with the Father, Son, Holy Spirit, with one another, and in the gospel (1 John 1:3,7; Phil. 3:10; Phil. 1:5). It speaks of Christians giving one another the right hand of fellowship (Gal. 2:9). The lack of fellowship in the church will kill evangelism. Jesus taught that our loving one another would show to the world that we belong to him. Christian fellowship is believers sharing their inner lives in the context of God's Word and in the power of the Holy Spirit.[1]

The third area in which the new converts were led by the apostles was called the "breaking of bread." They broke bread daily from house to house. You can't read the New Testament without hearing the rattle of dishes. The early believers liked to eat together and express their love for Christ and for each other. The Scripture says, "They were taking their meals together with gladness and sincerity of heart" (Acts 2:46). The word *sincerity* means free from rocks. They didn't have stony hearts, therefore they could have great fellowship.[2] They could have real love feasts.

Breaking the bread probably also included taking the Lord's Supper, the symbol of the death of Christ.

Fourth, the early believers participated with their apostle-teachers in prayer. Jesus had taught the apostles to pray; now they were teaching the early believers to pray. The apostles had prayed much before the coming of the Holy Spirit (Acts 1:14). Now all the believers had the help of the Holy Spirit in prayer (Rom. 8:26-27).

The early believers knew many lost people to pray for. They went to God in prayer before they went out into the world to witness. Prayer is essential for boldness in witnessing (Acts 4:29-32).

We who are interested in having evangelistic growth need to resolve with the early apostles to "devote ourselves to prayer, and the ministry of the Word" (Acts 6:4).

17

The Public Unexplainable Display of God's Power

Our God is the God of the unexplainable and the impossible. The angel said to Mary, "Nothing will be impossible with God" (Luke 1:37).

Christianity is a revelation of the unexplainable and the impossible. In early Christianity the Holy Spirit used the unexplainable to cause both the saved and the lost to have a deep sense of awe about the things of God (Acts 5:11).

Evangelistic growth in Acts pictures a repeated cycle of unexplainable happenings and a new surge in evangelistic growth.

Christ and the Unexplainable

Christ had a definite purpose in doing unexplainable things. When he performed his first miracle, the Scripture says that by it he "manifested His glory" (John 2:11). The word *glory* means that Christ was revealing himself as to who he is. He showed himself as the Messiah. He did things that only the Messiah could do.

The Scripture speaks of Christ's "signs" (John 2:11,23; 3:2; 4:54; 6:2,14,26,30; 7:31; 20:30). In John's Gospel the word is used seventeen times. It means an attesting miracle. The sense in which it is used shows the miraculous power of the deity of Jesus Christ. It was a visible pointer to the invisible truth about him. John indicated that he had selected certain signs that Jesus is the Son of

God (John 20:30). After Christ's first sign, the Scripture says that his disciples believed on him. The visible pointer served to confirm their faith. Christ's "signs" increased the faith of his friends and the hatred of his enemies.

Preaching and healing went together in Christ's ministry (Matt. 9:35). During the last week of his ministry he was still healing (Matt. 21:14-15).

Christ's signs not only proved that he was the Son of God (John 10:37-38), they drew large crowds so he could teach them about the kingdom of God (John 6:2).

Christ's raising of Lazarus shook the bastion of the Jewish religious system to its foundation. It served to force the hand of the Jewish religious leaders to either stand with him or reject him as the Messiah (John 12:17-19). The most irrefutable sign and the capstone of evangelistic growth was Christ's resurrection (Matt. 12:38-40).

Early Believers and the Unexplainable

Christ gave the twelve unexplainable power as he sent them out to proclaim the kingdom of God. He did the same thing to some seventy others (Luke 9:1-2; 10:1-9).

The early believers had the same purpose in performing "signs" as Jesus. They said it was by the power of Jesus that they performed their signs and that it proved he was the Messiah. In this context they called upon people to receive him as their Savior (Acts 4:10-12).

The apostles never claimed that they had power to heal or perform other miracles. The Bible says that the signs and wonders were taking place through the apostles, not by the apostles (Acts 2:43). When some men, who did not know Jesus personally, tried to perform miracles by his name, calamity fell upon them; and the name of Jesus was more highly magnified. A new surge of evangelistic growth occurred (Acts 19:13-20).

The unexplainable, done through the believers, caused masses to hear the gospel which resulted in multitudes being saved. The news spread about God striking two people dead, and "all the more believers in the Lord, multitudes . . . were constantly added" (Acts 5:14). Stephen performed wonders and signs, and a hostile crowd observed his face that glowed like an angel's. They heard him say that he saw Jesus standing at the right hand of God. This unexplainable happening had an indelible effect upon Paul (Acts 6:8,15; 7:55-58).

The Lord validated the preaching of Paul and Barnabas to both Jews and Greeks by "granting that signs and wonders be done by their hands" (Acts 14:3). The signs and wonders caused multitudes to become aware of Jesus and to hear him preached as the Messiah.

The writer of Hebrews says that the salvation that was first spoken of through the Lord was confirmed by God, granting signs and wonders and gifts of the Holy Spirit (Heb. 2:3-4). The God-given ability to heal is called a gift from the Holy Spirit (1 Cor. 12:9).

The Unexplainable and Evangelistic Growth Today

Amid the great awakenings that I read and hear about today, there is the phenomenon of the unexplainable. One of my former seminary classmates, who had attained unusual denominational leadership, experienced unexplainable healings in a 1981 revival crusade that was scheduled for one week but lasted many weeks.

My son, who is a member of a church that is experiencing unusual evangelistic growth, experienced healing. As a roofing contractor he had jarred his arm so much he had nerve damage and was losing the use of it. His doctor said it was nerve damage that could not be remedied. As he quietly prayed at the altar of his church, a strange warmth came to his arm. It was immediately healed, and he began to use it normally.

The Scripture says that "Jesus Christ is the same yesterday and today, yes and forever" (Heb. 13:8). Therefore, we know that he is capable today of doing, through his own, anything he wants to do.

I understand that amid the vast evangelistic growth in South Korea and South America the occurrence of signs and wonders is not unusual. Some of the leaders in the growth movement say that this attributes to the credibility of Jesus and to multitudes turning to him. The leaders also say there is a price to be paid by those whom the Lord chooses to perform his signs. People still become hostile in the presence of attesting miracles. Some people will not permit the Holy Spirit to convince them about Christ by any means.

After the Jewish council had heard the apostles preach Jesus as the Messiah, they threw them in jail. When the Lord took them out, by causing doors to lock and unlock and sentries to be passed without detecting any movement, the council was not convinced about Christ. Instead, they became more hostile toward those who preached him. Jesus said that the Father hid spiritual things from those who thought of themselves as wise and intelligent but revealed them to those who were as teachable as a little child (Luke 10:21). Nothing will convince some people about Jesus, but the Lord uses unexplainable "signs" to convince many.

There is a "sign" yet to be performed by the Lord. It is his second coming when every eye sees him. Until that time we should be open to permit him to perform through us attesting miracles if he so desires. "Signs" have a definite place in unexplainable evangelistic growth.

News of a spiritual happening that can't be explained in

terms of human ability will always get the world's attention. Let's permit the Holy Spirit to work in us and through us to perform any attesting miracle he desires that will awaken people to a felt need about Christ.

18

The Possessions Given to Meet Needs

Jesus said more about material things and a person's relation to them than he did about sin, salvation, heaven, and hell all grouped together.[1]

Many of the Christians who were saved on the Day of Pentecost stayed in the city of Jerusalem for some time to learn more about their newfound Messiah and Savior.[2] Sometime after their conversion, many of them began to be in physical need.

The disciples who had possessions would sell them and bring the money to the apostles to be shared with all in need. The money was not given simultaneously or under coercion. It was given from time to time as the need arose.[3] It was not communism. It was love on the part of believers who were able to meet a need and did so willingly (Acts 2:44-45). Two years following Pentecost their love for the Lord and for each other continued to be expressed in their selling and giving of their possessions (Acts 4:32-37). Satan tried to destroy the togetherness, and the consequent evangelistic growth, by enticing two members to lie about money. When the two fell dead, the church was purified again, and multitudes were added to its membership (Acts 5:1-14).

Biblical Basis for Giving Possessions

The first believers were Jewish. They had the Old Testament background and teaching on giving possessions.

First, they knew that all possessions belonged to God (Gen. 1:1; Pss. 24:1-2; 50:10-12).

Second, the early believers had been taught to honor the Lord with their wealth and from the first of their income (Prov. 3:9).

Third, through the last prophet before John, the Lord told the people that if they didn't bring tithes and offerings they were robbing him. However, if they would be faithful in their giving, they would be blessed by him (Mal. 3:10).

The early Christians believed that not only did their possessions belong to God, but they also belonged to him (1 Cor. 6:19-20).

The first believers had the teachings of Christ concerning giving. He had placed his approval on giving tithes (Matt. 23:23). He taught they should give in measure running over (Luke 6:38). He taught them to pay both taxes and tithes (Luke 20:25). During the last week of his life, he taught his apostles it was not how much a person gave but how much he had left over that was important (Mark 12:41-44).

Giving of Possessions Among Early Believers

The first believers gave out of a sense of fellowship and caring for each other. The Holy Spirit caused them to see that an exclusive personal ownership of material goods was not right. They had not brought anything into the world and would not take anything out of it. They saw grave danger in a possessive attitude toward wealth (1 Tim. 6:6-10). The unity rested on a ground of common faith and brought them into a sense of family feeling of common interest.[4] They acknowledged the lordship of Jesus in their giving. Their freedom in giving was related to their great power in witnessing (Acts 4:32-33).

The needs among the believers greatly affected their

giving with abandonment. Christ had taught them that their relationship to him in the way they responded to apparent needs among others would show up at the judgment (Matt. 25:34-40).

Principles of Giving for Early Believers

Second Corinthians 8—9 seems to summarize the principles of giving for a believer.

Giving should be a privilege granted by the grace of God. It should be liberal in the light of ability. It should be in addition to every other gracious work. It is a proof of genuine love. Christ's giving is to be an example for our giving. Every believer should participate on a basis of equality. The principle of bountiful sowing in order to have bountiful reaping should be kept in mind when one gives. Giving should be done not reluctantly or under compulsion, because God loves a cheerful giver. God is able to provide every need in abundance to those who give out of their faith. God will enrich the giver for his great generosity. Giving should be done with thankfulness for God's inexpressible gift, the Lord Jesus and our great salvation through him.

Pattern for New Testament Givers

The New Testament makes immorality and covetousness equally wrong (Col. 3:5). Covetousness is even called idol worship. Immediately following his magnanimous teaching on Christ's resurrection, Paul launched into teaching the pattern of giving for believers.

Giving is to be done on the first day of the week. This was the day Christ arose; it was the day of celebration for the early Christians; it was the day they met together.

Every believer is to participate in the giving. Giving is so important, it should be planned ahead of time.

Giving was to be according to how a person prospered. Proper giving, week by week, will prevent the need for some special offerings (1 Cor. 16:2).

Effect of Giving on Evangelistic Growth

The Scriptures teach that people cannot be saved unless they hear about Christ. They cannot hear about Christ without a preacher. Men cannot preach unless they are sent (Rom. 10:14-15). The word *sent* had the connotation of material support. This is a missionary plea for material support for missionaries. The Book of Philippians is a thank-you note to people who helped Paul financially in his preaching of the gospel.

The Scriptures teach that we should support people who carry the gospel as fellow workers with them. It says we do well to send—give material support—to people who are in God's service (1 John 3:6-8). To "send" the gospel is the privilege of the giver.

It takes an abandonment of self to have Christlike giving. The early Christians gave a good offering, because they first gave themselves to the Lord (2 Cor. 8:5). When the first church took care of the sticky problem of materialism, an amazing evangelistic growth followed (Acts 6:1-7).

Jesus taught that people could not serve things and the Lord at the same time; only one would be master. He also taught that if the things of God are put first, God would supply the material things that were needed (Matt. 6:24,33).

A strong witness and a covetous spirit are not found in the same believer. It is not unusual for those who trust God in the material realm to also trust him in the spiritual realm.

God wants missionaries sent, and he wants his preachers supported. He commanded that those who proclaimed the gospel get their livings from the gospel (1 Cor. 9:14).

The believer who would be evangelistic in thought and action must make available to his Lord all that he is and has. All ten tenths should be acknowledged as belonging to the Lord. One tenth should be dedicated as holy to him (Lev. 27:30). After this action by faith and love, the Christian is free to ask his Lord for the leading of the Holy Spirit to ascertain how much his offerings should be to the work of the Kingdom. The believer who dares to step out on faith to dedicate all that he has as belonging to the Lord, with a decision to use it to help others to come to know him, can be unusually used and blessed by the Lord.

For many years George Truett gave one week each year to preaching to cattlemen and their families in a canyon campsite in Texas. In a morning service he preached on the stewardship of giving. At the close a big cattleman came to him with a simple request, "Dr. Truett, will you follow me?"

The man turned to go down the floor of the canyon, and Dr. Truett followed. Soon they were winding up a trail that led to a high plateau. They stood and looked miles all around. Then the cattleman spoke for the second time. He explained that he had not been a Christian very long. He did not know until he heard Dr. Truett's sermon that all the land they could see did not belong to him, but to God. He also said that he did not know that all the cattle in sight were not his, but that they were God's.

Now that he had learned this he wanted Dr. Truett to kneel in the tall grass with him and tell the Lord that he dedicated it all to him. Then he said, "When you finish telling God that, you stop, because I want to tell him something."

Dr. Truett said they knelt, and he repeated to the Lord

what the cattleman had said. He acknowledged that all of his possessions were not really his; they belonged to God, and he'd try to use them for him. He would begin by giving the holy tenth to the Lord and then offerings far beyond as God blessed him.

Dr. Truett stopped praying and there was silence. The cattleman was breathing very deeply. Dr. Truett could tell he was highly agitated. Finally, the cattleman spoke, "Now God, you've heard what this preacher has said. I acknowledge all of this is yours, I give it to you. I dedicate it to you. And now, God, there is something else I want to give you."

The cattleman's voice broke, and there was silence except for his deep breathing. Finally, he spoke again in deep emotion. "Lord, what I want to give you is my son. He is wild and wicked. He is lost and on the way to hell. Lord, I give you my son. Amen."

Dr. Truett said they stood, and the cattleman turned and took the trail that led down to the floor of the canyon. They walked into the campground and parted for the afternoon. Evening came, and the people gathered for the night's service.

Dr. Truett said they had the song service, and then he stood to speak. He was only four or five minutes into his message when a voice rang out from the back, "Wait, wait." The voice was loud and urgent. People turned to look. Dr. Truett said he could see in the gathering twilight a figure skirting the audience, coming around to the right side, and up to the front where it stopped. A strong, young voice called to a big rancher sitting across on the other side and said, "Dad, Dad, I can't wait till this preacher stops to tell you that I have received Christ as my Savior."[5]

I do not need to tell you who's voice it was, and to whom he was speaking. God, in his strange and miraculous ways, will bless his children who dedicate their all to him and the work of his kingdom.

Evangelistic growth results at home and abroad when multitudes of God's people acknowledge the Lord and his gospel in their giving of material possessions.

19

The Praising of God
by His People

God's final and full revelation of himself in Jesus Christ was welcomed in songs of praise. Mary praised God that she was chosen to be the mother of the Savior (Luke 1:46-47). With praise the angels announced the birth of Christ as "good news of a great joy" (Luke 2:10). The shepherds returned from seeing him in the manger, "glorifying and praising God" (Luke 2:20). The Wise Men rejoiced exceedingly as they were given a star to guide them to him (Matt. 2:10). Two elderly people rejoiced and praised God when they recognized the Messiah in the baby Jesus (Luke 2:25-38).

Christianity is a singing religion. Even as his cross was approaching, Christ sang a hymn with his disciples.

Praising God is good for the individual Christian. It permits him to express his love for his Lord in warmth and emotion. The saved can also give the message of Christ to the lost through songs of praise. Churches with great celebrative singing are progressing, soul-winning churches. Singing the gospel is dynamic in a church's evangelistic growth.[1]

In a moment of ecstasy the church was born at Pentecost.[2] One of the participants later wrote "Is anyone cheerful? let him sing praises" (Jas. 5:13). Six months after Pentecost they were still "praising God" (Acts 2:47).

Praise in Hearts

Early Christians were "together with gladness and sincerity of heart (Acts 2:46)." The sincerity in their hearts meant they didn't have stony hearts; they had hearts of praise.

Robert Hamblin, evangelistic leader for the Southern Baptist Convention, says, "Christ in us is a triumphant hallelujah chorus. He is the song for our pilgrimage here."[3] Christ puts a song in the heart. I can never forget the joy that came into my heart when the Lord saved me.

The early believers were glad they'd come to know Jesus as the Messiah. Everywhere they took the message about him, joy sprang up in hearts. When Philip preached in Samaria, "There was much rejoicing in that city" (Acts 8:8). The Ethiopian went on his way rejoicing after he was saved (Acts 8:39). When the Philippian jailer and his household came to know the Lord, the Scripture says he rejoiced greatly (Acts 16:34).

Besides the knowledge of Christ there were other things that brought praise in the hearts of the early believers. They had received the gift of the Holy Spirit. They were enjoying a great fellowship. They were no longer just religious, they now had Christ. Praise welled up in their hearts.

Praise must have come to the early believers' hearts for the privilege of witnessing to their Savior. They were participants, not just observers. Every day they were witnessing to Christ in the Temple and in their homes. The witnessing life is the joyful life. The witnessing church is the praising church.

People who know Christ personally can "sing with the Spirit and . . . sing with the mind also" (1 Cor. 14:15).

Praise in Homes

As hearts are changed toward Christ, homes are changed. What great praises must have welled up in the Jerusalem homes as parents were saved and children came to know Christ, too. The early church met daily in homes, and the praise of their worship rang out in celebration.

Christians have an affinity for each other. They like to praise God together. When those early believers met, they had services of praise. The joy in their hearts and in their homes flooded over into their congregational meetings. In their home praise and in the Temple their joy and gladness was exposed to all who heard.

One of the ways a congregation praises God is through music and singing. Scripture tells the type of singing known to the early Christians. It was "psalms and hymns and spiritual songs" (Col. 3:16). The psalms were in their Scriptures. These probably composed most of their hymns. The "spiritual songs" were perhaps a kind of folk song with melodies of a highly emotional and exaltant character.[4]

It is interesting to note the direction of their praise. It was toward God, not toward men. Performance singing is toward men, praise singing is toward God. Possibly, one of the reasons church choirs are sometimes known as the "battleground of the church" is that some people are more interested in performing than in praising.

Congregational singing needs to be joyful and praising to have a positive effect for evangelistic growth. Praise in music has always had a vital part in evangelistic growth. Seemingly, every new upsurge in evangelistic growth and spiritual awakening in the last two hundred years has carried with it a new type of praise music acceptable to that generation. Many of the well-known evangelists had outstanding soloists and music directors who accompanied them on their evangelistic crusades.

A church that would win people to Christ in large numbers cannot have dull worship services. There is no room for boredom and coldness that chills and destroys evangelistic growth. One of the marks of growing churches is their evangelistic music. Music should never be for art's sake. It should be for the Lord's sake and for emphasizing evangelism.[5]

Even the invitation hymn needs to be sung with praise. A song that sounds like a dirge doesn't help the lost to decide for Christ.

Music should not only be filled with praise but be biblically sound, and present Christ as the Savior. No matter how good the music sounds, if the words do not magnify the Savior and point men to him the song has no place in Christian worship.

Sunday morning services, especially, should be alive and vibrant with praise. This is the one service that lost people are more likely to attend. If the church service is cold and stilted, and the music is not within the understanding of the congregation, lost people will stay away. In a service that is alive with praise to God, where the Holy Spirit is permitted to work with freedom among the people, the saved will rejoice, and the lost will turn to Christ.

Praise in Heaven

Christ said there is praise in heaven among the angels when one person turns from his sins to Christ. Praises must have rung continuously in heaven when the Jerusalem church won people daily to Christ.

Our congregational services today could well be patterned after the type of service we read about in heaven. It is celebrative. People are not afraid to raise their voices, and the person of Christ is magnified (Rev. 7:9-17).

Praise among the early believers reflected that they had accepted Christ's first priority as theirs. They wanted their loved ones and friends to know Christ. Their joy and praise for the Savior had a profound effect on those who did not know him. The Scripture says the people held them in high regard. Their joy and praise were contagious. Many turned to their Savior.

Services of praise will attract lost people today. Choirs that sing with celebration and praise in shopping malls, public beaches, and other places attract many for the Savior. A church that is filled with praises expressed in celebrative services will attract the lost in large numbers, and evangelistic growth can be rapid.

20

The People Outside
Highly Regarding God's People

People are the bottom line in evangelistic growth. People are the center of God's love. People brought Jesus from heaven. The church that walks in the will of God will be interested in winning people to Christ.

Christ cared for individuals. He also cared for the masses of people because they are composed of individuals. He was moved with compassion when he saw crowds that didn't know him (Matt. 9:36). He wanted to get to as many people as possible. He refused to stay in one place of popularity, saying that he had to go to other towns also. He told us to make disciples of all people everywhere.

The church that is truly interested in the people who are outside will find that those people will become interested in them. The early disciples took Christ's commission to reach people seriously. It was not long until the people outside began to regard them seriously.

Churches in America today are not persecuted, most are just ignored. There are reasons why the lost people in Jerusalem had high regard for the saved people.

First, the church had power to do things that outside people couldn't explain. When the Lord used Peter and John to heal a man who had never walked, the people outside gathered in large numbers to hear about the one who could heal. The Scripture says that it was "on account of the people" (Acts 4:21), and their high regard for the

Christians, that the Jewish leaders were afraid to punish the apostles. When things happen in the lives of people that cannot be explained in human terms, the world will take notice.

Second, it was a church that wouldn't tolerate flagrant sin among its people. When Peter challenged two people who were lying to the Holy Spirit, and they fell dead, the Scripture says, "The people held them in high esteem. And all the more believers in the Lord, multitudes of men and women, were constantly added to their number" (Acts 5:13-14). The church that calls for holy living on the part of its people will attract the outsider.

Third, a church that declares plainly and positively the whole message about the Lord will attract the outsider (Acts 5:20). People want a word of authority. They want to know what God says. The church that declares the whole doctrine of eternal life in Christ will be regarded as highly today as it was in Jerusalem. The outside people so highly regarded that church that the officers who were sent to arrest the leaders "were afraid of the people, lest they should be stoned" (Acts 5:26).

Fourth, the early church was attractive to people because the believers preached the forgiveness of sins (Acts 2:38; 3:19; 5:31).

Fifth, a church that believes in and follows her spiritual leadership is an attraction to people outside. The early believers had constantly devoted themselves to the apostles' teaching. They believed in their leaders. They followed their leaders. This impresses the outside world.

Sixth, a church where people love one another is attractive to the outsiders. The night before he died Jesus said that he was giving a new command "that you love one another, even as I have loved you" (John 13:34). Love for each other is not an option for God's children.

Christ said if we did love one another this would be a witness to the world that we belong to him. There is hunger in the world for love. It can best be found in the fellowship of true believers. In congregations where there's harmony, there's usually growth.

Seventh, the outside people were attracted to God's people because they declared an authoritative, positive message. The Messiah has abolished death and brought eternal life. People are interested in where they are going after death. People have a lurking fear of death. A church that preaches a certainty about an eternity with Christ will be attractive to outside people.

Bertha Smith, a former missionary to China and a well-known, spiritually awakening speaker, told me recently, "People are hungry for the Word of God. People everywhere are hungry for the Word. The pastor and church that preaches and teaches the Word will attract people." She was making the contrast between preachers and churches that just talk about the Word of God and those that really expound the Word of God. People were attracted to Jesus because he spoke with authority. The authority we have is in Jesus, in our personal experience with him, and in his Word. When God's people expound the Word, and their lives reflect the teaching of the Word, people will hunger for the Word.

Eighth, the first church attracted people because they went to the people. No human ability has ever been found that can reach more people for Christ, and reach them faster, than house-to-house visitation. As soon as the Scripture speaks of the early Christians going from house to house, with hearts of praise to God, it immediately speaks of them having favor with all the people. Then it tells how the Lord added to their number day by day. The church that is genuinely interested in people and will express this interest through prayer, personal testimony, and hard work may expect dramatic evangelistic growth. It was so in the days of the New Testament churches. It is so among our present-day churches.

Dr. Gaines S. Dobbins told in seminary class that soon after he became a professor in Louisville, they had a chapel speaker from another denomination. What he said reflects why some churches reach people while others do not. "When my denomination came to Louisville we asked, 'Where are our people?' When you Baptists came to Louisville you asked, 'Where are the people?' Today we have few churches, and you have many churches. We have reached a few people. You have reached many people."

How interested are you and your church in the people outside? How highly do the people outside regard your church? The answers to these questions may reveal why you are, or are not, experiencing evangelistic growth.

NOTES
Chapter 1
1. A. T. Robertson, *Word Pictures in the New Testament*, Vol. 3 (Nashville: Sunday School Board of the Southern Baptist Convention, 1930), p. 74.

2. Flavius Josephus, *The Life and Works of Josephus* (Chicago: The John C. Winston Company), p. 234,887.

Chapter 2
1. Robertson, p. 5.

2. Robertson, Vol. 1, p. 235.

3. William Barclay, *The Gospel of Luke* (Philadelphia: Westminster Press, 1953), p. 30.

Chapter 3
1. Richard B. Rackham, *The Acts of the Apostles* (London: Methuen & Company, 1901), p. 5.

2. W. O. Carver, *The Acts of the Apostles* (Nashville: Broadman Press, 1916), p. 13.

3. Herschel H. Hobbs, *An Exposition of the Four Gospels*, Vol. 4 (Nashville: Broadman Press, 1968), pp. 235-236.

Chapter 4
1. W. A. Criswell, "The Holy Spirit in Revival," *The Tie* (Southern Baptist Theological Seminary, March 1955), p. 3.

Chapter 5
1. A. T. Robertson, *Word Pictures in the New Testament*, Vol. 4 (Nashville: Sunday School Board of Southern Baptist Convention, 1931), p. 52.

2. Joseph Henry Thayer, *A Greek-English Lexicon of the New Testament* (New York: American Book Company, 1889), p. 245.

3. Robertson, pp. 9-10.

4. T. C. Smith, *The Broadman Bible Commentary*, Vol. 10 (Nashville: Broadman Press, 1970), p. 19.

5. Robert L. Maddox, Jr., "Layman's Bible Book Commentary," *Acts*, Vol. 19 (Nashville: Broadman Press, 1979), p. 21.

6. Leo Eddleman, *The Second Coming* (Nashville: Broadman Press, 1963), p. 89.

Chapter 6

1. R. B. Rackham, *The Acts of the Apostles* (London: Methuen & Company, 1901), p. 35.

2. Frank Cumpler. *Churches Alive and Growing* (Atlanta: Evangelism Section, Home Mission Board, Southern Baptist Convention), pp. 8-9.

Chapter 7

1. C. E. Autrey, *Evangelism in the Acts* (Grand Rapids: Zondervan Publishing House, 1964), p. 30.

2. *The Baptist Standard*, Texas Baptist Convention, November 1982, p. 7.

3. *Baptist Messenger*, Oklahoma Baptist State Convention, 15 April 1982, p. 5.

4. *The Baptist Standard*, 14 April 1982.

5. W. Stanley Mooneyham, *Christianity Today*, 18 September 1981, p. 20.

Chapter 8

1. A. T. Robertson, *Word Pictures in the New Testament*, Vol. 6 (Nashville: Sunday School Board of the Southern Baptist Convention, 1933), p. 159.

2. Harold Lindsell, *Christianity Today*, 1981, p. 16.

3. Ibid.

Chapter 9

1. A. T. Robertson, *Word Pictures in the New Testament*, Vol. 3 (Nashville: Sunday School Board of the Southern Baptist Convention, 1930), p. 20.

2. Tustin, "Red Hill Uses Shoppers," The California Southern Baptist, 1 April 1982, p. 5.

3. Robert H. Hill, "Believers Get a Taste of Evangelism," *Christianity Today*, 18 September 1981, p. 49.

Chapter 10
1. C. E. Autrey, *Evangelism in the Acts* (Grand Rapids: Zondervan Publishing House, 1964), p. 25.

Chapter 11
1. A. W. Goodwin Hudson, "The Methods of Group Evangelism," *Christianity Today,* 28 October 1966, p. 36.

Chapter 12
1. C. E. Autrey, *Evangelism in the Acts* (Grand Rapids: Zondervan Publishing House, 1964), p. 37.

2. Herschel H. Hobbs, *An Exposition of the Four Gospels,* Vol. 4 (Nashville: Broadman Press, 1968), p. 233.

Chapter 13
1. H. Franklin Paschall, *The Gospel for an Exploding World* (Nashville: Broadman Press, 1967), p. 82.

2. W. O. Carver, *The Acts of the Apostles* (Nashville: Broadman Press, 1916), p. 33.

3. A. T. Robertson, *Word Pictures in the New Testament,* Acts, Vol. 3 (Nashville: Sunday School Board of the Southern Baptist Convention, 1930), p. 34.

4. Robertson, Vol. 1, pp. 34-35.

Chapter 14
1. Roy J. Fish, *Giving a Good Invitation* (Nashville: Broadman Press, 1974), p. 11.

2. Leighton Ford, *The Christian Persuader* (New York: Harper & Row, 1966), p. 12.

3. Grady C. Cothen, *Unto All the World; Bold Mission* (Nashville: Broadman Press, 1979), p. 34.

Chapter 15
1. Herschel Hobbs, *An Exposition of the Four Gospels,* Vol. 1 (Nashville: Broadman Press, 1965), p. 36.

2. Joseph Henry Thayer, *A Greek-English Lexicon of the New Testament* (New York: American Book Company, 1889), p. 94.

3. Hobbs, p. 36.

4. A. T. Robertson, *Word Pictures in the New Testament,* Vol. 4

(Nashville: Sunday School Board of the Southern Baptist Convention, 1931), p. 298.

5. Ibid., p. 362.
6. Ibid., p. 493.

Chapter 16

1. Tim Phillips, *One Another* (Nashville: Broadman Press, 1981), p. 4.
2. A. T. Robertson, *Word Pictures in the New Testament*, Vol. 3, (Nashville: Sunday School Board of the Southern Baptist Convention, 1930), p. 40.

Chapter 18

1. Rudy Fagan, Unpublished Speech Made by the Executive Secretary of the Stewardship Commission of the Southern Baptist Convention to the West Virginia Convention of Southern Baptist Church Growth Conference, March 7, 1983.
2. W. O. Carver, *The Acts of the Apostles* (Nashville: Broadman Press, 1816), p. 35.
3. Ralph W. Neighbour, Jr., *Survival Kit for New Christians* (Nashville: Convention Press, 1982), p. 50.
4. Carver, p. 52.
5. George W. Truett, *A Quest for Souls* (Grand Rapids: Wm. B. Eerdman's Publishing Co., 1917), pp. 201-203.

Chapter 19

1. C. E. Matthews, *Southern Baptist Program of Evangelism* (Nashville: Convention Press, 1956), p. 151.
2. Hugh McElrath, "Music in the History of the Church," *Review and Expositor*, Spring 1972, p. 141.
3. Robert L. Hamblin, *Triumphant Strangers* (Nashville: Broadman Press, 1982), p. 98.
4. McElrath, 142.
5. Don Hustad, "Teaching Ministers," *The Tie*, March-April 1983, p. 13.